TExES
238
Life Science 7-12
Teacher Certification Exam

By: Sharon Wynne, M.S.

XAMonline, INC.
Boston

XAMonline, Inc.
21 Orient Ave.
Melrose, MA 02176
Toll Free 1-800-301-4647
Email: info@xamonline.com
Web www.xamonline.com
Fax: 1-617-583-5552

Library of Congress Cataloging-in-Publication Data

Wynne, Sharon
    Life Science 7-12 (238): Teacher Certification / . -4th ed.
    ISBN 978-1-60787-376-1
    1. Life Science 7-12 (238).   2. Study Guides.   3. TExES
    4. Teachers' Certification & Licensure.   5. Careers

Disclaimer:

The material presented in this publication is the sole work of XAMonline and was created independently from the National Education Association, Educational Testing Service, or any State Department of Education, National Evaluation Systems or other testing affiliates.

Between the time of publication and printing, state-specific standards, testing formats, and website information may change. XAMonline developed the sample test questions and they reflect similar content to that found on actual tests; however, they are not former tests. XAMonline assembles content that aligns with state standards, but makes no claims nor guarantees regarding test performance. Numerical scores are determined by testing companies such as NES or ETS and then are compared with individual state standards. A passing score varies from state to state.

Printed in the United States of America œ-1

TExES: Life Science 7-12 (238)
ISBN: 978-1-60787-376-1

Table of Contents

Great Study and Testing Tips!

What to study in order to prepare for the subject assessments is the focus of this study guide, but equally important is *how* you study.

You can increase your chances of truly mastering the information by taking some simple, but effective steps.

Study Tips:

1. Some foods aid the learning process. Foods such as milk, nuts, seeds, rice, and oats help your study efforts by releasing natural memory enhancers called CCKs (*cholecystokinins*) composed of *tryptophan*, *choline*, and *phenylalanine*. All of these chemicals enhance the neurotransmitters associated with memory. Before studying, try a light, protein-rich meal of eggs, turkey, and fish. All of these foods release memory enhancing chemicals. The better the connections, the more you comprehend.

Likewise, before you take a test, stick to a light snack of energy-boosting and relaxing foods. A glass of milk, a piece of fruit, or some peanuts all release various memory-boosting chemicals and help you relax and focus on the subject at hand.

2. Learn to take great notes. A by-product of our modern culture is that we have grown accustomed to getting our information in short doses (e.g., TV news sound bites or USA Today style newspaper articles).

Consequently, we've subconsciously trained ourselves to assimilate information better in neat little packages. If your notes are scrawled all over the paper, it fragments the flow of the information. Strive for clarity. Newspapers use a standard format to achieve clarity. Your notes can be much clearer through use of proper formatting. A very effective format is called the *"Cornell Method."*

> Take a sheet of loose-leaf lined notebook paper and draw a line all the way down the paper about 1-2" from the left-hand edge.

> Draw another line across the width of the paper about 1-2" up from the bottom. Repeat this process on the reverse side of the page.

Look at the highly effective result. You have ample room for notes, a left hand margin for special emphasis items or inserting supplementary data from the textbook, a large area at the bottom for a brief summary, and a little rectangular space for just about anything you want.

3. <u>**Get the concept then the details.**</u> Too often we focus on the details and fail to gather an understanding of the concept. If you simply memorize dates, places, and names, you may well miss the whole point of the subject.

Putting concepts in your own words can increase your understanding. If you are working from a textbook, automatically summarize each paragraph in your mind. If you are outlining text, don't simply copy the author's words, *rephrase* them in your own words.

You remember your own thoughts and words much better than someone else's, and when you summarize in your own words you subconsciously tend to associate the important details to the core concepts.

4. <u>**Ask "Why?"**</u> Pull apart written material paragraph by paragraph and don't forget the captions under the illustrations.

Example: If the heading is "Stream Erosion", flip it around to read "Why do streams erode?" Then answer the question.

If you train your mind to think in a series of questions and answers, not only will you learn more, but you will decrease your test anxiety by increasing your familiarity with the question and answer process.

5. <u>**Read for reinforcement and future needs.**</u> Even if you only have ten minutes, put your notes or a book in your hand. Your mind is similar to a computer; you have to input data in order to process it. *By reading, you are creating the neural connections for future retrieval.* The more times you read something, the more you reinforce the learning of ideas.

Even if you don't fully understand something on the first pass, *your mind stores much of the material for later recall.*

6. <u>**Relax to learn.**</u> Our bodies respond to an inner clock called biorhythms. Burning the midnight oil works well for some people, but not everyone.

If possible, set aside a particular place to study that is free of distractions. Shut off the television, cell phone, and pager and "exile" your friends and family during your study period.

If silence really bothers you, try background music. Light classical music at a low volume has been shown to aid in concentration. Music that evokes pleasant emotions without lyrics is highly suggested. Try just about anything by Mozart. It relaxes you.

7. Use arrows not highlighters. At best, it's difficult to read a page full of yellow, pink, blue, and green streaks. Try staring at a neon sign for a while and you'll soon see that the horde of colors obscures the message.

A quick note, a brief dash of color, an underline, and an arrow pointing to a particular passage is much clearer than a horde of highlighted words.

8. Budget your study time. Although you shouldn't ignore any of the material, *allocate your available study time in the same ratio that topics may appear on the test.*

Testing Tips:

1. Get smart, play dumb. Don't read anything into the question. Don't make an assumption that the test writer is looking for something else than what is asked.

2. Read the question and all the choices *twice* before answering the question. You may miss something by not carefully reading and re-reading both the question and the answers.

If you really don't have a clue as to the right answer, leave it blank on the first time through. Go on to the other questions, as they may provide a clue as to how to answer the skipped questions.

If, later on, you still can't answer the skipped ones—*guess.* The only penalty for guessing is that you *might* get it wrong. One thing is certain; if you don't put anything down, you *will* get it wrong.

3. Turn the question into a statement. Look at the wording of the questions. The syntax of the question usually provides a clue. Does it seem more familiar as a statement rather than as a question? Does it sound strange?

By turning a question into a statement, you may be able to spot if an answer sounds right, and it may also trigger memories of material you have read.

4. Look for hidden clues. It's actually very difficult to compose multiple-foil (choice) questions without giving away part of the answer in the options presented.

In most multiple-choice questions you can often readily eliminate one or two of the potential answers. This leaves you with only two real possibilities and automatically your odds go to fifty-fifty with very little work.

5. Trust your instincts. On questions that you aren't really certain about, go with your basic instincts. **Your first impression on how to answer a question usually is correct.**

6. Mark your answers directly on the test booklet. Don't bother trying to fill in the optical scan sheet on the first pass through the test.

Just be very careful not to miss-mark your answers when you eventually transcribe them to the scan sheet.

7. Watch the clock! You have a set amount of time to answer the questions. Don't get bogged down trying to answer a single question at the expense of 10 questions you can more readily answer.

DOMAIN I.   SCIENTIFIC INQUIRY AND PROCESSES

Competency 001   The teacher understands how to select and manage learning activities to ensure the safety of all students and the correct use and care of organisms, natural resources, materials, equipment, and technologies.

Laboratory safety procedures

All science labs should contain the following **safety equipment**.

- Fire blanket that is visible and accessible
- Ground Fault Circuit Interrupter (GFCI) equipped power outlets when within two feet of water supplies
- Signs designating room exits
- Emergency shower providing a continuous flow of water
- Emergency eye wash station that can be activated by the foot or forearm
- Eye protection for every student
- A means of sanitizing equipment
- Emergency exhaust fans providing ventilation to the outside of the building
- Master cut-off switches for gas, electric, and compressed air. Switches must have permanently attached handles. Cut-off switches must be clearly labeled
- An ABC fire extinguisher
- Storage cabinets for flammable materials
- Chemical spill control kit
- Fume hood with an extraction motor that is spark proof
- Protective laboratory aprons made of flame-retardant material
- Signs that will alert of potential hazardous conditions
- Labeled containers for broken glassware, flammables, corrosives, and waste

Students should wear safety goggles when performing dissections, heating anything, or while using acids and bases. Hair should always be tied back and objects should never be placed in the mouth. Food should not be consumed while in the laboratory. Hands should always be washed before and after laboratory experiments. In case of an accident, eye washes and showers should be used for eye contamination or a chemical spill that covers the student's body. Small chemical spills should only be contained and cleaned by the teacher.

Kitty litter or a chemical spill kit should be used to clean a spill. For large spills, the school administration and the local fire department should be notified. Biological spills should only be handled by the teacher. Contamination with biological waste can be cleaned by using bleach when appropriate. Accidents and injuries should always be reported to the school administration and local health facilities. The severity of the accident or injury will determine the course of action.

It is the responsibility of the teacher to provide a safe environment for his or her students. Proper supervision greatly reduces the risk of injury and a teacher should never leave a class for any reason without providing alternate supervision. After an accident, two factors are considered, **foreseeability** and **negligence**. Foreseeability is the anticipation that an event may occur under certain circumstances. Negligence is the failure to exercise ordinary or reasonable care. Safety procedures should be a part of the science curriculum and a well-managed classroom is important to avoid potential lawsuits.

Storing, identifying, and disposing of chemicals and biological materials

All laboratory solutions should be prepared as directed in the lab manual. Care should be taken to avoid contamination. All glassware should be rinsed thoroughly with distilled water before using and well cleaned after use. All solutions should be made with distilled water as tap water contains dissolved particles that may affect the results of an experiment. Unused solutions should be disposed of according to local disposal procedures.

Various "Right to Know" laws cover science teachers who work with potentially hazardous chemicals. Briefly, the laws state that employees must be informed of potentially toxic chemicals. An inventory must be maintained and made available if requested. The inventory must contain information about the hazards and properties of the chemicals. This inventory is to be checked against the "Substance List". Training must be provided on safe handling and interpretation of Material Safety Data Sheets.

The following chemicals are potential carcinogens and are not allowed in school facilities: Acrylonitrile, Arsenic compounds, Asbestos, Benzidine, Benzene, Cadmium compounds, Chloroform, Chromium compounds, Ethylene oxide, Ortho-toluidine, Nickel powder, and Mercury.

Chemicals should not be stored on bench tops or near heat sources. They should be stored in groups based on their reactivity with one another and in protective storage cabinets. All containers within the lab must be labeled. Suspected and known carcinogens, when allowed, must be labeled as such and stored in trays to contain leaks and spills.

Chemical waste should be disposed of only in properly labeled containers. Waste should be separated based on its reactivity with other chemicals.

Biological material should never be stored near food or water used for human consumption. All biological material should be appropriately labeled. All blood and body fluids should be put in a well-contained container with a secure lid to prevent leaking. All biological waste should be disposed of in biological hazardous waste bags.

Material safety data sheets (MSDS) are available for every chemical and biological substance. These are available directly from the distribution company and the internet. Before using lab equipment, all lab workers should read and understand the equipment manuals.

Use of live specimens

No dissections may be performed on living mammalian vertebrates or birds. Lower order life and invertebrates may be used. Biological experiments may be done with all animals except mammalian vertebrates or birds. No physiological harm may result to the animal. All animals housed and cared for in the school must be handled in a safe and humane manner. Animals are not to remain on school premises during extended vacations unless adequate care is provided. Any instructor who intentionally refuses to comply with the laws may be suspended or dismissed.

Pathogenic organisms must never be used for experimentation. Students should adhere to the following rules at all times when working with microorganisms to avoid accidental contamination:

1. Treat all microorganisms as if they were pathogenic.
2. Maintain sterile conditions at all times.

Dissection and alternatives to dissection

Animals which were not obtained from recognized sources should not be used for dissection. Decaying animals or those of unknown origin may harbor pathogens and/or parasites. Specimens should be rinsed before handling. Latex gloves are recommended. If gloves are not available, students with sores or scratches should be excused from the activity. Formaldehyde is likely carcinogenic and should be avoided or disposed of according to district regulations. Students objecting to dissections for moral reasons should be given an alternative assignment. Interactive dissections are available online or from software companies for those students who object to performing dissections. There should be no penalty for those students who refuse to physically perform a dissection.

Knowledge of appropriate use of laboratory materials

Light microscopes are commonly used in high school laboratory experiments. Total magnification is determined by multiplying the magnification of the ocular and the objective lenses. Oculars usually magnify 10X and objective lenses usually magnify 10X on low and 40X on high.

Procedures for the care and use of microscopes include:

- clean all lenses with lens paper only
- carry microscopes with two hands (one on the arm and one on the base)
- always begin on low power when focusing in before switching to higher power
- store microscopes with the low power objective down
- always use a coverslip when viewing wet mount slides bring the objective down to its lowest position when focusing, then move up to higher position
- avoid breaking the slide or scratching the lens

Wet mount slides should be made by placing a drop of water on the specimen and then putting a glass coverslip on top of the drop of water. Dropping the coverslip at a forty-five degree angle will help avoid air bubbles.

Chromatography refers to a set of techniques that are used to separate substances based on their different properties such as size or charge. Paper chromatography uses the principles of capillarity to separate substances such as plant pigments. Molecules of a larger size will move more slowly up the paper, whereas smaller molecules will move more quickly producing lines of pigment.

An **indicator** is any substance used to assist in the classification of another substance. An example of an indicator is litmus paper. Litmus paper is a way to measure whether a substance is acidic or basic. Blue litmus turns pink when an acid is placed on it and pink litmus turns blue when a base is placed on it. pH paper is a more accurate measure of pH, with the paper turning different colors depending on the pH value.

Spectrophotometry measures percent of light at different wavelengths absorbed and transmitted by a pigment solution.

Centrifugation involves spinning substances at a high speed. The more dense part of a solution will settle to the bottom of the test tube, where the lighter material will stay on top. Centrifugation is used to separate blood into blood cells and plasma, with the heavier blood cells settling to the bottom.

Electrophoresis uses electrical charges of molecules to separate them according to their size. The molecules, such as DNA or proteins, are pulled through a gel towards either the positive end of the gel box (if the material has a negative charge) or the negative end of the gel box (if the material has a positive charge). DNA is negatively charged and moves towards the positive end.

One of the most widely used genetic engineering techniques is the **polymerase chain reaction (PCR)**. PCR is a technique in which a piece of DNA can be amplified into billions of copies within a few hours. This process requires a primer to specify the segment to be copied, and an enzyme to amplify the DNA.

PCR has allowed scientists to perform multiple procedures on small amounts of DNA.

The metric system

Science uses the **metric system** (or SI system), as it is accepted worldwide and allows easy comparisons among experiments done by scientists around the world.

The meter is the basic metric unit of length. One meter is approximately 1.1 yards. The liter is the basic metric unit of volume. 3.785 liters is 1 gallon. The gram is the basic metric unit of mass. One thousand grams (a kilogram) is approximately 2.2 pounds.

The following prefixes define multiples of the basic metric units.

Prefix	Multiplying factor	Prefix	Multiplying factor
deca-	10X the base unit	deci-	1/10 the base unit
hecto-	100X	centi-	1/100
kilo-	1,000X	milli-	1/1,000
mega-	1,000,000X	micro-	1/1,000,000
giga-	1,000,000,000X	nano-	1/1,000,000,000
tera-	1,000,000,000,000X	pico-	1/1,000,000,000,000

Length is the distance from one point to another. The SI unit of length is the meter (m). One thousand meters make 1 kilometer (km).

Volume is the amount of space a substance occupies. The SI unit of volume is the liter (L).

Mass is the amount of matter in an object. The SI unit of mass is the gram (g). There are 1,000 grams in a kilogram.

Time is the period between two events. In SI, time is measured in seconds.

Temperature is a measure of heat in something. The SI scale for measuring temperature is the Kelvin scale (K). However, in most sciences, temperature is measured in Celsius because it is an easier scale for ordinary use.

Appropriate measuring devices

A common instrument used for measuring volume is the graduated cylinder. A typical unit of measurement is the milliliter (mL). To ensure accurate measurement, it is important to read the liquid in the cylinder at the bottom of the **meniscus**, the curved surface of the liquid.

A common instrument used in measuring mass is the triple beam balance. The triple beam balance can accurately measure tenths of a gram and can estimate hundredths of a gram.

The ruler and meter stick are the most commonly used instruments for measuring length. As with all scientific measurements, standard units of length are metric.

Competency 002 **The teacher understands the nature of science, the process of scientific inquiry, and the unifying concepts that are common to all sciences.**

Similarities among systems in math, science, and technology

Math, science, and technology share many common themes. All three use models, diagrams, and graphs to simplify concepts for analysis and interpretation. Patterns observed in these systems lead to predictions based on these observations. Another common theme among these three systems is equilibrium. **Equilibrium** is a state in which forces are balanced, resulting in stability. Static equilibrium is stability due to a lack of changes, and dynamic equilibrium is stability due to a balance between opposing forces.

Processes by which hypotheses are generated and tested

Science is a body of knowledge systematically derived from study, observations, and experimentation. Its goal is to identify and establish principles and theories that may be applied to solve problems. Pseudoscience, on the other hand, refers to beliefs that are not supported by hard evidence. In other words, there is no scientific methodology or application involved with pseudoscience. Some classic examples of pseudoscience include witchcraft, alien encounters, or any topic explained by hearsay.

Scientific experimentation must be repeatable. Experimentation results in theories that can be disproved and changed. Science depends on communication, agreement, and disagreement among scientists. It is composed of hypothesis, theories, and laws.

Hypothesis - An unproved theory or an "educated guess" followed by research to best explain a phenomena. A theory is a proven hypothesis.

Theory - A statement of principles or relationships relating to a natural event or phenomenon, which have been verified by experimentation and accepted as correct by most scientists.

Law - An explanation of events that occur with uniformity under the same conditions (e.g., laws of nature, law of gravitation). Laws often are difficult to test experimentally but are generally accepted by scientists.

Science often is limited by the available technology. An example of this would be the relationship between the invention of the microscope and the discovery of the cell. As our technology improves, allowing better experimentation, more hypotheses will become theories. Data collection methods also limit scientific inquiry. Data may be interpreted differently on different occasions. Limitations of scientific methodology produce explanations that change as new technologies emerge.

The first step in scientific inquiry is posing a question. Next, a hypothesis is formed to provide a plausible explanation. An experiment is then proposed and performed to test this hypothesis. A comparison between the predicted and observed results is the next step. Conclusions are then formed and it is determined whether the hypothesis is correct or incorrect. If incorrect, the next step is to form a new hypothesis and repeat the process. This process often is referred to as the "scientific method".

Methods or procedures for collecting data

The procedure used to obtain data is important to the outcome. Experiments consist of **controls** and **variables**. A control is the experiment run under normal, non-manipulated conditions.

A variable is a factor or condition the scientist manipulates. In biology, the variable may be light, temperature, pH, time, etc. Scientists can use the differences in tested variables to make predictions or form hypotheses. Only one variable should be tested at a time. In other words, one would not alter both the temperature and pH of the experimental subject.

An **independent variable** is one is the researcher directly changes or manipulates. This could be the amount of light given to a plant or the temperature at which bacteria is grown. The **dependent variable** is the factor that changes due to the influence of the independent variable; generally, the dependent variable is the object of the experimentation.

Knowledge of appropriate and effective graphic representation of data

The type of graphic representation used to display observations depends on the type of data being presented. **Line graphs** compare different sets of related data and help predict data. For example, a line graph could compare the rate of activity of different enzymes at varying temperatures. A **bar graph** or **histogram** compares different groupings of items and helps make comparisons based on the data groups. For example, a bar graph could compare the ages in months of children in a classroom. A **pie chart** is useful when organizing data as part of a whole. For example, a pie chart could display the percent of time students spend on various after school activities.

Knowledge of labeling graphs with independent and dependent variables

As previously noted, the researcher controls the independent variable. The independent variable usually is placed on the x-axis (horizontal axis). The dependent variable is influenced by the independent variable and is placed on the y-axis (vertical axis). It is important to choose the appropriate units for labeling the axes. It is best to divide the largest value to be plotted by the number of blocks on the graph, and round to the nearest whole number.

Competency 003 The teacher understands the history of science, how science impacts the daily lives of students, and how science interacts with and influences personal and societal decisions.

The impact of social factors on biological study

Society, as a whole, impacts biological research. For example, the pressure from the majority of society has led to restrictions on human cloning research. The United States government and the governments of many other countries have restricted human cloning. The U.S. legislature has banned the use of federal funds for the development of human cloning techniques. Some individual states have banned human cloning regardless of where funding originates.

The societal and industrial demand for increased productivity of crops has steadily increased over the years. Genetic engineering in the agricultural field has led to improved crops and increased yields for human use and consumption. Crops are genetically modified for increased growth and insect resistance because of the demand for larger and greater quantities of produce.

Advances in biotechnology are often opposed by some segments of society. Ethical questions come into play when discussing animal and human research. Does it need to be done? What are the effects on humans and animals? There are no absolute right or wrong answers to these questions. There are governmental agencies in place to regulate the use of humans and animals for research.

Science and technology are often referred to as a "double-edged sword". Although advances in medicine have greatly improved the quality and length of life, certain moral and ethical controversies have arisen. Unforeseen environmental problems may result from technological advances. Advances in science have led to enhanced health practices, yet it has caused the cost of medical care to skyrocket. Society depends on science, yet it is necessary that the public be scientifically literate and informed in order to allow meaningful debate. Especially vulnerable are the areas of genetic research and fertility. It is important for science teachers to stay abreast of current research and to involve students in critical thinking and ethical consideration whenever possible.

DOMAIN II. CELL STRUCTURE AND PROCESSES

Competency 004 **The teacher understands the structure and function of biomolecules.**

Compare and contrast hydrogen, ionic, and covalent bonds

Chemical bonds form when atoms with incomplete valence shells share or transfer their valence electrons. There are three types of chemical bonds: covalent bonds; ionic bonds; and hydrogen bonds.

Covalent bonding is the sharing of a pair of valence electrons by two atoms. A simple example of this is two hydrogen atoms bonded as a hydrogen molecule. Each hydrogen atom has one valence electron in its outer shell, therefore the two hydrogen atoms come together to share their electrons. Some atoms share two pairs of valence electrons, like two oxygen atoms. This is called a double covalent bond.

The attraction for the electrons of a covalent bond is called electronegativity. The greater the electronegativity of an atom, the more it pulls the shared electrons towards itself. Electronegativity of the atoms determines whether the bond is polar or nonpolar. In **nonpolar covalent bonds**, the electrons are shared equally, thus the electronegativity of the two atoms is the same. This type of bonding usually occurs between two atoms of the same element. A **polar covalent bond** forms when different atoms join, like when hydrogen and oxygen bond to create water. In this case, oxygen is more electronegative than hydrogen so the oxygen pulls the hydrogen electrons toward itself.

[handwritten margin note, left:] - no charges - two same nonmetals

[handwritten margin note, right:] - partial ionic charges - two different nonmetals

Ionic bonds form when one electron is stripped away from its atom to join another atom. An example of this is sodium chloride (NaCl). A single electron on the outer shell of sodium joins the chloride atom with seven electrons in its outer shell. The sodium now has a +1 charge and the chloride now has a -1 charge. The charges attract each other to form an ionic bond. Ionic compounds are called salts. In a dry salt crystal, the bond is so strong it requires a great deal of strength to break it apart. But, place the salt crystal in water, and the bond dissolves easily as the attraction between the two atoms decreases.

[handwritten margin note, left:] - full ionic charges - metal + nonmetal

The weakest of the three bonds is the **hydrogen bond**. A hydrogen bond forms when one electronegative atom partially shares a hydrogen atom with another electronegative atom. An example of a hydrogen bond is a water molecule (H_2O) bonding with an ammonia molecule (NH_3). The H^+ atom of the water molecule attracts the negatively charged nitrogen in a weak bond. Weak hydrogen bonds are beneficial because they can briefly form, the atoms can respond to one another, and then break apart allowing formation of new bonds. Hydrogen bonding, though generally very transient, plays a very important role in the chemistry of life.

Analyze the structure and function of carbohydrates, lipids, proteins, and nucleic acids

A compound consists of two or more elements. There are four major groups of chemical compounds found in the cells and bodies of living things. These are carbohydrates, lipids, proteins, and nucleic acids.

Monomers are the simple unit of structure. **Monomers** combine to form **polymers**, or long chains of repeating monomers, to make a large variety of molecules. Monomers combine through the process of condensation reactions (also called dehydration synthesis). In this process, one molecule of water is removed between each of the adjoining molecules. In order to break the molecules apart in a polymer, water molecules are added between monomers, thus breaking the bonds between them. This process is called hydrolysis.

Carbohydrates contain a ratio of two hydrogen atoms for each carbon and oxygen $(CH_2O)_n$. Carbohydrates include sugars and starches. They function in the storage and release of energy. **Monosaccharides** are the simplest sugars and include glucose, fructose, and galactose. They are major nutrients for cells. In cellular respiration, the cells extract the energy from glucose molecules. **Disaccharides** (polymers) are made by joining two monosaccharides (monomers) by condensation to form a glycosidic linkage (covalent bond between two monosaccharides). Maltose is the combination of two glucose molecules, lactose is the combination of glucose and galactose, and sucrose is the combination of glucose and fructose.

Polysaccharides (polymers) consist of many monomers joined together. They are storage material hydrolyzed as needed to provide sugar for cells or building material for structures protecting the cell. Examples of polysaccharides include starch, glycogen, cellulose, and chitin.

- **Starch** - major energy storage molecule in plants. It is a polymer consisting of glucose monomers.
- **Glycogen** - major energy storage molecule in animals. It is made up of many glucose monomers.

- **Cellulose** - found in plant cell walls, its function is structural. Many animals lack the enzymes necessary to hydrolyze cellulose, so it simply adds bulk (fiber) to the diet.

- **Chitin** - found in the exoskeleton of arthropods and fungi. Chitin contains an amino sugar (glycoprotein).

Lipids are composed of glycerol (an alcohol) and three fatty acids. Lipids are **hydrophobic** (water fearing) and will not mix with water. There are three important families of lipids, fats, phospholipids, and steroids.

- **Fats** consist of glycerol (alcohol) and three fatty acids. Fatty acids are long carbon skeletons. The nonpolar carbon-hydrogen bonds in the tails of fatty acids are highly hydrophobic. Fats are solids at room temperature and come from animal sources (e.g., butter and lard).

- **Phospholipids** are a vital component in cell membranes. In a phospholipid, one or two fatty acids are replaced by a phosphate group linked to a nitrogen group. They consist of a **polar** (charged) head that is hydrophilic (water loving) and a **nonpolar** (uncharged) tail which is hydrophobic. This allows the membrane to orient itself in a bilayer with the polar heads facing the interstitial fluid found outside the cell and the nonpolar tails facing the nonpolar tails of the "other side" of the bilayer.

- **Steroids** are insoluble and are composed of a carbon skeleton consisting of four inter-connected rings. An important steroid is cholesterol, which is the precursor from which other steroids are synthesized. Hormones, including cortisone, testosterone, estrogen, and progesterone, are steroids. Their insolubility keeps them from dissolving in body fluids.

Proteins compose about fifty percent of the dry weight of animals and bacteria. Proteins function in structure and support (e.g., connective tissue, hair, feathers, and quills), storage of amino acids (e.g., albumin in eggs and casein in milk), transport of substances (e.g. hemoglobin), coordination of body activities (e.g. insulin), signal transduction (e.g. membrane receptor proteins), contraction (e.g. muscles, cilia, and flagella), body defense (e.g. antibodies), and as enzymes to speed up chemical reactions.

All proteins (polymers) are made of twenty **amino acids** (monomers). An amino acid contains an amino group and an acid group. The amino group varies and determines the type of the amino acid. Amino acids form proteins through condensation reactions with the removal of water. The bond formed between two amino acids is called a peptide bond. Polymers of amino acids are called polypeptide chains (generally, proteins). An analogy can be drawn between the twenty amino acids and the alphabet. We can form millions of words using an alphabet of only twenty-six letters. Similarly, organisms can create many different proteins using the twenty amino acids. This results in the formation of many different proteins, whose structure defines the function.

There are four levels of protein structure: primary, secondary, tertiary, and quaternary.

Primary structure is the protein's unique sequence of amino acids. A slight change in primary structure can affect a protein's conformation (geometry) and its ability to function. **Secondary structure** refers to the coils (alpha helixes) and folds (pleated sheets) of polypeptide chains. The coils and folds are the result of hydrogen bonding along the polypeptide backbone. The secondary structure is either in the form of an alpha helix or a pleated sheet. The alpha helix is a coil held together by hydrogen bonds. A pleated sheet is the polypeptide chain folding back and forth. The hydrogen bonds between parallel regions hold it together. **Tertiary structure** is formed by hydrogen bonding between the side chains of the amino acids. For example, disulfide bridges form when two sulfhydryl groups on the amino acids bond together to form a stable hydrogen bond. **Quaternary structure** is the overall structure of the protein from the aggregation of two or more polypeptide chains. An example of this is hemoglobin. Hemoglobin consists of two each of two kinds of polypeptide chains.

Nucleic acids consist of DNA (deoxyribonucleic acid) and RNA (ribonucleic acid).

Nucleic acids contain the code for the amino acid sequence of proteins and the instructions for self-replication. The monomer of nucleic acids is a nucleotide. A nucleotide consists of a 5-carbon sugar (deoxyribose in DNA, ribose in RNA), a phosphate group, and a nitrogenous base. The base sequence is the code or the instructions. There are five bases: adenine, thymine, cytosine, guanine, and uracil. Uracil is found only in RNA and replaces thymine, found only in DNA. The following provides a summary of nucleic acid structure:

	SUGAR	PHOSPHATE	BASES
DNA	Deoxyribose	Present	adenine, **thymine**, cytosine, guanine
RNA	Ribose	Present	adenine, **uracil**, cytosine, guanine

Due to the molecular structure, adenine will always pair with thymine in DNA or uracil in RNA. Cytosine always pairs with guanine in both DNA and RNA.

This allows for the symmetry of the DNA molecule seen below.

DNA

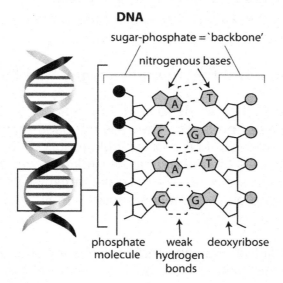

Adenine and thymine (or uracil) are linked by two hydrogen bonds and cytosine and guanine are linked by three hydrogen bonds. Guanine and cytosine are harder to break apart than thymine (uracil) and adenine because of the greater number of bonds between the bases. The double-stranded DNA molecule forms a double helix, or twisted ladder, shape.

Analyze the properties of water and its significance to living organisms

Water is necessary for life. The unique properties of water are due to its molecular structure. Water is an important solvent in biological compounds. Water is a polar substance. This means it is formed by covalent bonds that make it electrically lopsided (polar covalent bonds).

Water molecules are attracted to other water molecules due to this electrical attraction and this allows for two important properties: adhesion and cohesion. Adhesion is when water sticks to other substances like the xylem of a stem, which aids the water in traveling up the stem to the leaves. Cohesion is the ability of water molecules to stick to each other by hydrogen bonding. This allows for surface tension on a body of water, or capillarity, which allows water to move through vessels. Surface tension is a measure of how difficult it is to stretch or break the surface of a liquid. Cohesion allows water to move against gravity.

There are several other important properties of water. Water is a good solvent. An aqueous solution is one in which water is the solvent. It provides a medium for chemical reactions to occur. Water has a high specific heat of 1 calorie per gram per degree Celsius, allowing it to cool and warm slowly, allowing organisms to adapt to temperature changes. Water has a high boiling point; thus, it is a good coolant. Its ability to evaporate stabilizes the environment and allows organisms to maintain their body temperature. Water has a high freezing point and a lower density as a solid than as a liquid. Water is most dense at four degrees Celsius. This means ice floats on top of water so a whole body of water does not freeze during the winter. Because of this property of water, aquatic organisms can survive the winter under the ice.

Analyze the structure and function of enzymes and factors

Enzymes act as biological catalysts to speed up reactions. Enzymes are the most diverse of all types of proteins. They are not used up in a reaction and are recyclable. Each enzyme is specific for a single reaction. Enzymes act on a substrate. The substrate is the material to be broken down or put back together. Most enzymes end in the suffix *-ase* (e.g. lipase, amylase). The prefix often is the substrate being acted on (e.g. maltase acts on maltose,). This convention is not used for all enzymes, however.

Each enzyme has an active site—the region of the enzyme that binds to the substrate. There are two theories for how the active site functions. The **lock and key theory** states that the shape of the enzyme is specific because it fits into the substrate like a key fits into a lock. It aids in holding molecules close together so reactions can easily occur. The **Induced fit theory** states that an enzyme can stretch and bend to fit the substrate. This is the most accepted theory.

Many factors can affect enzyme activity. Temperature and pH are two of those factors. The temperature can affect the rate of reaction of an enzyme. The optimal pH for most enzymes is between 6 and 8, with a few enzymes whose optimal pH falls out of this range.

Cofactors aid in the enzyme's function. Cofactors may be inorganic or organic. Organic (carbon containing) cofactors are known as coenzymes. Vitamins are examples of coenzymes. Some chemicals can inhibit an enzyme's function. **Competitive inhibitors** block the substrate from entering the active site of the enzyme to reduce productivity. **Noncompetitive inhibitors** bind to the enzyme in a location not in the active site but still interrupt substrate binding. In most cases, noncompetitive inhibitors alter the shape of the enzyme. An **allosteric enzyme** can exist in two shapes; they are active in one form and inactive in the other. Overactive enzymes may cause metabolic diseases.

Competency 005   The teacher understands that cells are the basic structures of living things and have specialized parts that perform specific functions.

Distinguish between prokaryotes and eukaryotes

The cell is the basic unit of all living things. There are three types of cells: prokaryotic, eukaryotic, and archaea. Archaea have some similarities with prokaryotes, but are as distantly related to prokaryotes as prokaryotes are to eukaryotes.

Prokaryotes

Prokaryotes consist only of bacteria and cyanobacteria (formerly known as blue-green algae). The diagram below shows the classification of prokaryotes.

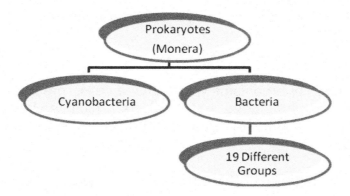

Bacterial cells have no defined nucleus or nuclear membrane. The DNA, RNA, and ribosomes float freely within the cell. The cytoplasm has a single chromosome condensed to form a **nucleoid**. Many prokaryotes have a thick cell wall made up of amino sugars (glycoproteins) that provides protection, gives the cell shape, and keeps the cell from bursting. The antibiotic penicillin targets the **cell wall** of bacteria. Penicillin works by disrupting the cell wall, thus killing the cell.

The cell wall surrounds the **cell membrane** (plasma membrane). The cell membrane consists of a lipid bilayer that controls the passage of molecules in and out of the cell. Some prokaryotes have a capsule made of polysaccharides that surrounds the cell wall for extra protection.

Many bacterial cells have appendages used for movement called **flagella**. Some cells also have **pili**, which are protein strands used for attachment. Pili may also be used for sexual conjugation (where bacterial cells exchange DNA).

Prokaryotes are the most numerous and widespread organisms on earth. Bacteria were most likely the first cells and date back in the fossil record to 3.5 billion years ago. Their ability to adapt to the environment allows them to thrive in a wide variety of habitats.

Eukaryotes

Eukaryotic cells are found in protists, fungi, plants, and animals. Most eukaryotic cells are larger than prokaryotic cells. They contain many organelles, which are membrane bound areas for specific functions. Eukaryotic cytoplasm contains a cytoskeleton which provides a protein framework for the cell. The cytoplasm also supports the organelles and contains the ions and molecules necessary for cell function. The cytoplasm is contained by the plasma membrane. The plasma membrane some allows molecules to pass in and out of the cell but prevents other molecules from doing so—it is semi-permeable. The membrane can bud inward to engulf outside material in a process called endocytosis. Exocytosis is a secretory mechanism, the reverse of endocytosis.

Archaea

There are three kinds of organisms with archaea cells: **methanogens**, obligate anaerobes that produce methane, **halobacteria**, which can live only in concentrated brine solutions, and **thermoacidophiles**, which can live only in acidic hot springs.

Compare and contrast archaea, prokaryotes, and eukaryotes

The most significant difference between prokaryotes and eukaryotes is that eukaryotes have a **nucleus**. The nucleus is the "brain" of the cell that contains all of the cell's genetic information. The chromosomes consist of chromatin, which are complexes of DNA and proteins. The chromosomes are tightly coiled to conserve space while providing a large surface area. The nucleus is the site of transcription of the DNA into RNA. The **nucleolus**, a region inside the nucleus, is where ribosomes are made. There is at least one of these dark-staining bodies inside the nucleus of most eukaryotes. The nuclear envelope consists of two membranes separated by a narrow space. The envelope contains many pores that let RNA out of the nucleus.

Archaea, prokaryotes, and eukaryotes all have ribosomes. Only eukaryotes have more complex organelles including the endoplasmic reticulum, Golgi complex, lysosomes, mitochondria, and plastids. These eukaryotic organelles are explained in more detail in the parts of eukaryotic cells, below.

The Endosymbiotic Theory proposes that mitochondria and chloroplasts were once free living and possibly evolved from prokaryotic cells. At some point in our evolutionary history, they entered the eukaryotic cell and maintained a symbiotic relationship with the cell, with both the cell and organelle benefiting from the relationship. The fact that they both have their own DNA, RNA, ribosomes, and are capable of reproduction supports this theory.

The following is a diagram of a generalized animal cell.

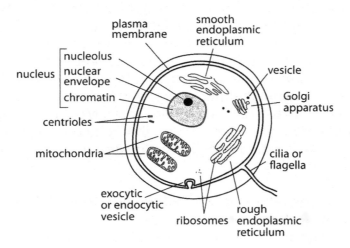

Analyze the structure and processes of prions and viruses

Microbiology includes the study of monera, protists, and viruses. Although **viruses** are not classified as living things, they greatly affect other living things by disrupting cell activity. Viruses are obligate parasites because they rely on the host for their own reproduction. Viruses are composed of a protein coat and a nucleic acid, either DNA or RNA. A bacteriophage is a virus that infects a bacterium. Animal viruses are classified by the type of nucleic acid, presence of RNA replicase, and presence of a protein coat.

There are two types of viral reproductive cycles:

1. **Lytic cycle** - The virus enters the host cell and makes copies of its nucleic acids and protein coats and reassembles. It then lyses or breaks out of the host cell and infects other nearby cells, repeating the process.

2. **Lysogenic cycle** - The virus may remain dormant within the cell untilsome factor activates it and stimulates it to break out of the cell. Herpes is an example of a lysogenic virus.

Prions are protein fibrils that contain no DNA or RNA. Prions cause scrapie in sheep and bovine spongiform encephalitis ("mad-cow" disease) in cows. This disease is characterized by destruction of neural tissue resulting in a sponge-like brain. Prions also cause slow developing disease of the nervous system in humans similar to those in animals. Kreutzfeldt-Jacob Syndrome and kuru are two of the human diseases caused by prions. Prion diseases are contracted by consuming the tissue of infected organisms.

Compare archaebacteria and eubacteria

Archaebacteria and eubacteria are the two main branches of prokaryotic (moneran) evolution. Archaebacteria evolved from the earliest cells. Most achaebacteria inhabit extreme environments. There are three main groups of archaebacteria: methanogens, extreme halophiles, and extreme thermophiles. Methanogens are strict anaerobes, extreme halophiles live in high salt concentrations, and extreme thermophiles live in hot temperatures (hot springs). Generally speaking, archaebacteria are fairly rare. Most prokaryotes fall into the eubacteria (bacteria) domain. Bacteria are divided according to their morphology (shape). Bacilli are rod-shaped bacteria, cocci are round bacteria, and spirilli are spiral-shaped bacteria.

Gram negative
-pink
-lipopolysaccharides

Gram positive
- purple
-peptidoglycan

The Gram stain is a procedure used to differentiate the cell wall make-up of bacteria. Gram positive bacteria have simple cell walls consisting of large amounts of peptidoglycan. These bacteria pick up the stain, revealing a purple color when observed under the microscope. Gram negative bacteria have a more complex cell wall consisting of less peptidoglycan, but have large amounts of lipopolysaccharides. The lipopolysaccharides resist the stain, revealing a pink color when observed under the microscope. Because of the lipopolysaccharide cell wall, Gram negative bacteria tend to be more toxic and are more resistant to antibiotics and host defense mechanisms.

Bacteria reproduce by binary fission. This asexual process is simply dividing the bacterium in half. Both new organisms are exact clones of the parent.

Bacteria locomotion, called taxi, is performed via flagella. Taxis is the movement towards or away from a stimulus. The methods for obtaining nutrition are, for photosynthetic organisms or producers, the conversion of sunlight to chemical energy; and for consumers or heterotrophs, consumption of other living organisms; and, for saprophytes, consumption of dead or decaying material.

In comparison, archaebacteria contain no peptidoglycan in the cell wall, they are not inhibited by antibiotics, they have several kinds of RNA polymerase, and they do not have a nuclear envelope. Eubacteria (bacteria) have peptidoglycan in the cell wall, they are susceptible to antibiotics, they have one kind of RNA polymerase, and they have no nuclear envelope.

Structure and function of protists

Protists are the earliest eukaryotic descendants of prokaryotes. Protists are found almost anywhere there is water. Protists, a very large group of disparate organisms, can be broadly defined as eukaryotic microorganisms that include the macroscopic algae with only a single tissue type. They are defined by exclusion of characteristics common to the other kingdoms. They are not prokaryotes because they have (usually) a true nucleus and membrane-bound organelles. They are not fungi because fungi lack undulopidia and develop from spores. They are not plants because plants develop from embryos, and they are not animals because animals develop from a blastula.

Most protists have a true (membrane-bound) nucleus, complex organelles (mitochondria, chloroplasts, etc.), aerobic respiration in mitochondria, and undulipodium (cilia) in some life stage.

The chaotic status of names and concepts of the higher classification of the protists reflects their great diversity of form, function, and life cycles. The protists are often grouped as algae (plant-like), protozoa (animal-like), or fungus-like, based on the similarity of their lifestyle and characteristics to these more clearly defined groups. Two distinctive groups of protists are sometimes considered for separation into their own kingdoms. The Archaezoa lack mitochondria, the Golgi apparatus, and have multiple nuclei. The Chromista, including diatoms, brown algae, and "golden" algae with chlorophyll c, have a very different photosynthetic plastid from those found in the green algae and plants.

Knowledge of the significance of fungi, bacteria, and viruses

Although bacteria and fungi may cause disease, they are also beneficial for use as medicines and food. Penicillin is derived from a fungus that is capable of destroying the cell wall of bacteria. Many antibiotics work in this way. Some antibiotics can interfere with bacterial DNA replication or can disrupt the bacterial ribosome without affecting the host cells. Viral diseases have been fought through the use of vaccination, where a small amount of the virus is introduced so the immune system is able to recognize it upon later infection. Antibodies are more quickly manufactured when the host has had prior exposure. Finally, researchers often use viruses and retroviruses as vectors for the delivery of genes to bacteria, plants, and animals in genetic engineering processes (e.g., gene therapy, creation of transgenic organisms).

The majority of prokaryotes decompose material for use by the environment and other organisms. The eukaryotic fungi are the most important decomposers in the biosphere. They break down organic material to be used up by other living organisms. The fungi are characterized by a short lived diploid stage, which cannot be viewed except under a microscope. The structures that are visible to the naked eye are typically puffballs, mushrooms, and shelf fungi that represent the dikaryote form of the fungi. The haploid stages are commonly observed as the absorptive hyphae or as asexual reproductive sporangia.

Identify cell organelles and their functions

Parts of Eukaryotic Cells

1. Nucleus - The "brain" of the cell. The nucleus contains:

> **Chromosomes** - DNA, RNA, and proteins tightly coiled to conserve space while providing a large surface area.

> **Chromatin** - loose structure of chromosomes. Chromosomes are found in the form of chromatin when the cell is not dividing.

> **Nucleoli** - where ribosomes are made. These are seen as dark spots in the nucleus.

> **Nuclear membrane** - contains pores which let RNA out of the nucleus. The nuclear membrane is continuous with the endoplasmic reticulum which allows the membrane to expand or shrink if needed.

2. Ribosomes - the site of protein synthesis. Ribosomes may be free-floating in the cytoplasm or attached to the endoplasmic reticulum. There may be up to a half a million ribosomes in a cell, depending on how much protein the cell makes.

3. Endoplasmic Reticulum - this large membranous structure is highly folded and provides a large surface area. These folds are the "roadways" of the cell and allow for transport of materials within the cell and out of the cell. The lumen, or interior, of the endoplasmic reticulum helps to keep materials isolated from the cytoplasm and headed in the right direction. The endoplasmic reticulum is capable of building new membrane material. There are two types of endoplasmic reticulum:

- **Smooth Endoplasmic Reticulum** - contains no ribosomes on its surface.

- **Rough Endoplasmic Reticulum** - contains ribosomes on its surface. This form of ER is abundant in cells that make many proteins, such as pancreas cells, which produce many digestive enzymes.

4. Golgi Complex or Golgi Apparatus - this is a stacked disc structure with extensive surface area. The Golgi Complex functions to sort, modify, and package molecules that are made in other parts of the cells. These molecules are either sent out of the cell or to other organelles within the cell.

5. Lysosomes - found mainly in animal cells. These contain digestive enzymes that break down food, unnecessary substances, viruses, damaged cell components, and eventually the cell itself.

6. Mitochondria - large organelles that make ATP to supply energy to the cell. Muscle cells have many mitochondria because they use a great deal of energy. Mitochondria have a double membrane, and the inner membrane is highly folded. The folds inside the mitochondria are called cristae. They provide a large surface area for the reactions of cellular respiration to occur. Mitochondria have their own DNA and are capable of reproducing themselves if there is a great demand for additional energy.

7. Plastids - found in photosynthetic organisms only. They are similar to the mitochondria inasmuch as they have a double membrane structure. They also have their own DNA and can reproduce if the need for the increased photosynthetic activity becomes necessary. There are several types of plastids:

- **Chloroplasts** – green in color, function in photosynthesis. They are capable of trapping the energy sunlight and converting it into chemical energy.

- **Chromoplasts** - make and store yellow and orange pigments; they incidentally provide color to leaves, flowers and fruits.

- **Amyloplasts** - store starch and are used as a food reserve. They are abundant in roots and tubers like potatoes.

8. Cell Wall - found in plant cells almost exclusively, the cell wall is composed of cellulose and fibers. It is thick enough for support and protection, yet porous enough to allow water and dissolved substances to enter. Cell walls are cemented to each other.

9. Vacuoles - hold stored water, food, and pigments. Vacuoles are very large in plants. This quality allows them to fill with water in order to provide turgor pressure. Lack of turgor pressure causes a plant to wilt.

10. Cytoskeleton - composed of protein filaments attached to the plasma membrane and organelles. The cytoskeleton provides a framework for the cell and aids in cell movement. Unlike an animal skeleton, the cytoskeleton constantly changes shape and moves about. Three types of fibers make up the cytoskeleton:

- **Microtubules** - largest of the three filaments, and also makes up cilia and flagella for locomotion. Flagella grow from a basal body. Some examples are sperm cells and tracheal cilia. Centrioles are also composed of microtubules and form the spindle fibers that pull the cell apart into two cells during cell division. Centrioles are not found in the cells of higher plants.

- **Intermediate Filaments** - they are smaller than microtubules but larger than microfilaments. They help the cell to keep its shape.

- **Microfilaments** - smallest of the three fibers, they are made of actin and small amounts of myosin (like in muscle tissue). They function in cell movement like cytoplasmic streaming, endocytosis, and amoeboid movement. Microfilaments pinches the two daughter cells apart after cell division, forming two new cells.

Identify cell types, structures, and functions

Animal cells – Importantly, animal cells have a nucleus, or a round body inside the cell, which controls the cell's activities. The nuclear membrane contains threadlike structures called chromosomes. The genes are units that control cell activities found in the nucleus. The cytoplasm hosts many structures. Vacuoles contain the food for the cell. Other vacuoles contain waste materials. Animal cells differ from plant cells because they do not have plastids or a cell wall.

Plant cells – Unique from animal cells, plant cells have cell walls. A cell wall differs from a cell membrane. The cell membrane is very thin and is a part of the cell. The cell wall is thick and is a non-living part of the cell. Chloroplasts are other structures found in plant cells but not in animal cells. They are little bundles of chlorophyll.

Single cells – A single-cell organism is called a **protist.** When you look under a microscope the animal-like protists are called **protozoans.** They do not have chloroplasts. They are usually classified by the way they move about looking for food. For example, amoebas engulf other protists by flowing around and over them.

The paramecium has a hair-like structure that allows it to move back and forth, appearing in action like tiny oars, searching for food. The euglena is an example of a protozoan that moves with a tail-like structure called a flagella.

Competency 006   The teacher understands how cells carry out life processes.

Understand the importance of active and passive transport

In order to understand cellular transport, it is important to know about the structure of the cell membrane. All organisms contain cell membranes that regulate the flow of materials into and out of the cell. The current model for the cell membrane is the Fluid Mosaic Model, which takes into account the ability of lipids and proteins to move and change places, giving the membrane fluidity.

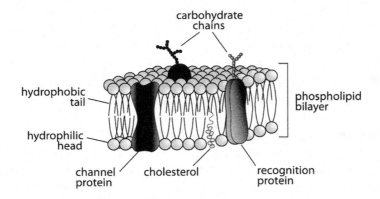

Cell membranes have the following characteristics:

1. They are made of phospholipids which have polar, charged heads with a phosphate group which is hydrophilic (water loving) and two nonpolar lipid tails which are hydrophobic (water fearing). This allows the membrane to orient itself with the polar heads facing the fluid inside and outside the cell and the hydrophobic lipid tails sandwiched in between. Each individual phospholipid is called a micelle. This double layer of phospholipids is often called the phospholipid bilayer.

2. They contain proteins embedded inside (integral proteins) and proteins on the surface (peripheral proteins). These proteins may act as channels for transport, may contain enzymes, may act as receptor sites, may act to stick cells together, or may attach to the cytoskeleton to give the cell shape.

3. They contain cholesterol, which alters the fluidity of the membrane.

4. They contain oligosaccharides (small carbohydrate polymers) on the outside of the membrane. These act as markers that help distinguish one cell from another.

5. They contain receptors made of glycoproteins that can attach to certain molecules, like hormones.

Cell transport is necessary to maintain homeostasis, or balance between the cell and its external environment. Cell membranes are selectively permeable, which is the key to transport. Not all molecules may pass through easily. Some molecules require energy or carrier molecules and may only cross when needed.

Passive transport does not require energy and moves the material with the concentration gradient (high to low). Small molecules may pass through the membrane in this manner. Two examples of passive transport include diffusion and osmosis. **Diffusion** is the ability of molecules to move from areas of high concentration to areas of low concentration. It normally involves small uncharged particles like oxygen. **Osmosis** is simply the diffusion of water across a semi-permeable membrane. Osmosis may cause cells to swell or shrink, depending on the internal and external environments. The following terms are used to describe the relationship of the cell to the environment.

Isotonic - Water concentration is equal inside and outside the cell. Net movement in either direction is basically equal.

Hypertonic - "Hyper" refers to the amount of dissolved particles. The more particles are in a solution, the lower its water concentration. Therefore, when a cell is hypertonic to its environment, there is more water outside the cell than inside. Water will move into the cell and the cell will swell. If the environment is hypertonic to the cell, there is more water inside the cell. Water will move out of the cell and the cell will shrink.

Hypotonic - "Hypo" again refers to the amount of dissolved particles. The fewer particles are in solution, the higher its water concentration. When a cell is hypotonic to its environment, there is more water inside the cell than outside. Water will move out of the cell and the cell will shrink. If the environment is hypotonic to the cell, there is more water outside the cell than inside. Water will move into the cell and the cell will swell.

The **facilitated diffusion** mechanism does not require energy, but does require a carrier protein. An example is insulin, which is needed to carry glucose into the cell.

Active transport requires energy. The energy for this process comes from either ATP or an electrical charge difference. Active transport may move materials either with or against a concentration gradient. Some examples of active transport are:

- Sodium-Potassium pump - maintains an electrical difference across the cell membrane. This is useful in restoring ion balance so nerves can continue to function. It exchanges sodium ions for potassium ions across the plasma membrane in animal cells.

- Stomach acid pump - exports hydrogen ions to lower the pH of the stomach and increase acidity.

- Calcium pumps - actively pump calcium outside of the cell and are important in nerve transmission and muscle function.

Active transport involves a membrane potential, which is a charge on the membrane. The charge works like a magnet and may cause transport proteins to alter their shape, thus allowing substances in or out of the cell.

The transport of large molecules depends on the fluidity of the membrane, which is controlled by cholesterol in the membrane. **Exocytosis** is the release of large particles by vesicles fusing with the plasma membrane. In the process of **endocytosis**, the cell takes in macromolecules and particulate matter by forming vesicles derived from the plasma membrane. There are three types of endocytosis in animal cells. **Phagocytosis** is when a particle is engulfed by pseudopodia and packaged in a vacuole. In **pinocytosis**, the cell takes in extracellular fluid in small vesicles. **Receptor-mediated endocytosis** is when the membrane vesicles bud inward to allow a cell to take in large amounts of certain substances. The vesicles have proteins with receptors that are specific for the substance.

Understand the significance of photosynthesis and respiration to living organisms

Glycolysis is the first step in respiration. It occurs in the cytoplasm of the cell and does not require oxygen. Each of the ten stages of glycolysis is catalyzed by a specific enzyme. The following is a summary of these stages.

In the first stage the reactant is glucose. For energy to be released from glucose, it must be converted to a reactive compound. This conversion occurs through the phosphorylation of a molecule of glucose by the use of two molecules of ATP. This is an investment of energy by the cell. The 6-carbon product, called fructose-1,6-bisphosphate, breaks into two 3-carbon molecules. A phosphate group is added to each sugar molecule and hydrogen atoms are removed. Hydrogen is picked up by NAD^+ (an electron carrier). Since there are two halves of the sugar molecule, two molecules of NADH are formed.

As the phosphate bonds are broken, ATP is produced. Two ATP molecules are generated as each original 3-carbon sugar molecule is converted to pyruvic acid (pyruvate). A total of four ATP molecules are made in the four stages. Since two molecules of ATP were needed to start the reaction in the initial stage, there is a net gain of two ATP molecules at the end of glycolysis. This accounts for only about two percent of the total energy in a molecule of glucose.

Assuming that oxygen is present in the cellular environment, beginning with pyruvate, which was the end product of glycolysis, the following steps occur before entering the **Krebs cycle**.

1. Pyruvic acid is changed to acetyl-CoA (coenzyme A). This is a 3-carbon pyruvic acid molecule which has lost one atom of carbon to become a 2-carbon acetyl group. Pyruvic acid loses a hydrogen atom to NAD^+, which is reduced to NADH.

2. Acetyl CoA enters the Krebs cycle. For each molecule of glucose entering glycolysis, two molecules of Acetyl CoA enter the Krebs cycle (one for each molecule of pyruvic acid formed in glycolysis).

The **Krebs cycle** (also known as the citric acid cycle), occurs in four major steps. First, the 2-carbon acetyl CoA combines with a 4-carbon molecule to form a 6-carbon molecule of citric acid. Next, two carbons are lost and a 4-carbon molecule is formed to become available to join with CoA to form citric acid again. Since we started with two molecules of CoA, two turns of the Krebs cycle are necessary to process the original molecule of glucose. In the third step, eight hydrogen atoms are released and picked up by FAD and NAD^+ (electron carriers). Lastly, for each molecule of CoA (remember there were two to start with) you get:

> 3 molecules of NADH x 2 cycles
> 1 molecule of $FADH_2$ x 2 cycles
> 1 molecule of ATP x 2 cycles

Therefore, this completes the breakdown of glucose. At this point, a total of four molecules of ATP have been made, two from glycolysis and one from each of the two turns of the Krebs cycle. Six carbon atoms have been released, two prior to entering the Krebs cycle and two for each of the two turns of the Krebs cycle. Twelve carrier molecules have been made, ten NADH and two $FADH_2$. These carrier molecules will carry electrons to the electron transport chain.

ATP is made by substrate-level phosphorylation in the Krebs cycle. Notice that the Krebs cycle in itself does not produce much ATP, but functions mostly in the transfer of electrons to be used in the electron transport chain that makes the most ATP.

In the **Electron Transport Chain,** NADH transfers electrons from glycolysis and the Kreb's cycle to the first molecule in the chain of molecules embedded in the inner membrane of the mitochondrion.

Most of the molecules in the electron transport chain are proteins. Nonprotein molecules are also part of the chain and are essential for the catalytic functions of certain enzymes. The electron transport chain does not make ATP directly.

Instead, it breaks up a large free energy drop into a more manageable one. The chain uses highly energetic electrons to pump H^+ ions across the mitochondrial membrane. The H^+ gradient thus established is used to form ATP synthesis in a subsequent process called **chemiosmosis** (oxidative phosphorylation). ATP synthetase and energy generated by the movement of hydrogen ions coming off of NADH and $FADH_2$ builds ATP from ADP on the inner membrane of the mitochondria. Each NADH yields three molecules of ATP (10 x 3) and each $FADH_2$ yields two molecules of ATP (2 x 2). Thus, the electron transport chain and oxidative phosphorylation produces about 34 ATP.

Thus, the net gain from the whole process of respiration is 36 molecules of ATP:

Process	# ATP produced (+)	# ATP consumed (-)	Net # ATP
Glycolysis	4	2	+2
Acetyl CoA	0	2	-2
Krebs cycle	1 per cycle (2 cycles)	0	+2
Electron transport chain	34	0	+34
Total			+36

Photosynthesis is an anabolic process that stores energy in the form of a three carbon sugar. We will use glucose as an example for this section.

Photosynthesis occurs only in organisms that contain chloroplasts (i.e., plants, some bacteria, and some protists). There are a few terms to be familiar with when discussing photosynthesis.

An **autotroph** (self-feeder) is an organism that makes its own food from the energy of the sun or other elements. Autotrophs include:

1. **photoautotrophs** - make food from light and carbon dioxide, releasing oxygen that can be used for respiration.

2. **chemoautotrophs** - oxidize sulfur and ammonia. Some bacteria are chemoautotrophs.

Heterotrophs ("other feeders") are organisms that must eat other living things to obtain energy. Another term for heterotrophs is **consumers**. All animals are heterotrophs. **Decomposers** break down once-living things. Bacteria and fungi are examples of decomposers. **Scavengers** eat dead things. Examples of scavengers are bacteria, fungi, and some animals.

The **chloroplast** is the site of photosynthesis. It shares a similar structure to the mitochondria and inside has a greatly increased surface area of the thylakoid membrane. It also contains a fluid called stroma between and around the stacks of thylakoids. The thylakoid membrane contains pigments (chlorophyll) that are capable of capturing light energy.

Photosynthesis essentially reverses the electron flow discussed above in the electron transport chain. Water is split by the chloroplast into hydrogen and oxygen. The oxygen is given off as a waste product as carbon dioxide is reduced to sugar (glucose). This requires the input of energy, which comes from the sun.

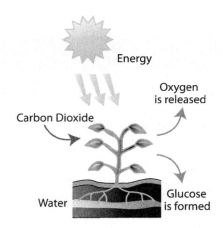

Photosynthesis occurs in two main stages, the light reactions and the Calvin cycle (dark reactions). The conversion of solar energy to chemical energy occurs in the light reactions. Electrons are transferred by the absorption of light by chlorophyll and cause the water to split, releasing oxygen as a waste product. The chemical energy created in the light reaction is in the form of NADPH. ATP is also produced by a process called photophosphorylation. These forms of energy are produced in the thylakoids and are used in the Calvin cycle to produce sugar.

The second stage of photosynthesis is the **Calvin cycle**. Carbon dioxide in the air is incorporated into organic molecules already in the chloroplast. The NADPH produced in the light reaction is used as reducing power for the reduction of the carbon to carbohydrate. ATP from the light reaction is also needed to convert carbon dioxide to carbohydrate (sugar).

The two stages of photosynthesis are depicted below.

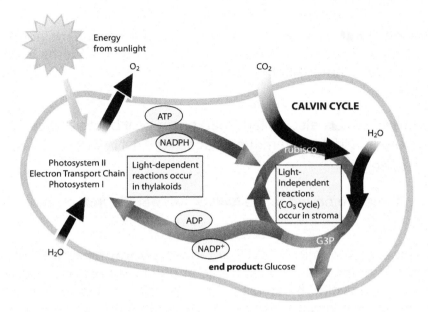

The process of photosynthesis is made possible by the presence of the sun. Visible light ranges in wavelengths of 750 nanometers (red light) to 380 nanometers (violet light). As wavelength decreases, the amount of available energy increases. Light is carried as photons, which are fixed quantities of energy. Light is reflected (what we see), transmitted, or absorbed (what the plant uses). The plant's pigments capture light of specific wavelengths. Remember that the light that is reflected is what we see as color. Plant pigments include:

Chlorophyll *a* - reflects green/blue light; absorbs red light
Chlorophyll *b* - reflects yellow/green light; absorbs red light
Carotenoids - reflects yellow/orange; absorbs violet/blue light

The pigments absorb photons. The energy from the light excites electrons in the chlorophyll that jump to orbitals with more potential energy and reach an "excited" or unstable state.

The basic chemical formula for photosynthesis is:

$$CO_2 + H_2O + \text{energy (from sunlight)} \circledast C_6H_{12}O_6 + O_2$$

The high energy electrons are trapped by primary electron acceptors which are located on the thylakoid membrane. These electron acceptors and the pigments form reaction centers called photosystems that are capable of capturing light energy. Photosystems contain a reaction-center chlorophyll that releases an electron to the primary electron acceptor. This transfer is the first step of the light reactions.

There are two photosystems, named according to their date of discovery, not their order of occurrence.

1. **Photosystem I** is composed of a pair of chlorophyll *a* molecules. Photosystem I is also called P700 because it best absorbs light of 700 nanometers. Photosystem I makes ATP whose energy is needed to build glucose.

2. **Photosystem II** is also called P680 because it best absorbs light of 680 nanometers. Photosystem II produces ATP + $NADPH_2$ and the waste gas oxygen.

Both photosystems are bound to the **thylakoid membrane**, close to the electron acceptors.

The photosynthetic production of ATP is termed **photophosphorylation** due to the use of light. Photosystem I uses cyclic photophosphorylation because the pathway occurs in a cycle. It can also use noncyclic photophosphorylation which starts with light and ends with glucose. Photosystem II uses noncyclic photophosphorylation only.

Below is a diagram of the relationship between cellular respiration and photosynthesis.

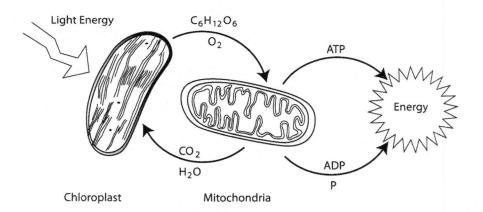

Compare aerobic and anaerobic respiration

Glycolysis generates ATP with oxygen (aerobic) or without oxygen (anaerobic). We have already discussed aerobic respiration. Anaerobic respiration can occur by fermentation. ATP can be generated by fermentation by substrate level phosphorylation if there is enough NAD^+ present to accept electrons during oxidation. In anaerobic respiration, NAD^+ is regenerated by transferring electrons to pyruvate. There are two common types of fermentation.

In **alcoholic fermentation**, pyruvate is converted to ethanol in two steps. In the first step, carbon is released from the pyruvate. In the second step, ethanol is produced by the reduction of acetaldehyde by NADH. This results in the regeneration of NAD$^+$ for glycolysis. Alcohol fermentation is carried out by yeast and some bacteria.

Pyruvate is reduced to form lactate as a waste product by NADH in the process of **lactic acid fermentation.** Animal cells and some bacteria that do not use oxygen utilize lactic acid fermentation to make ATP. Lactic acid forms when pyruvic acid accepts hydrogen from NADH. A buildup of lactic acid is what causes muscle soreness following exercise.

Energy remains stored in the lactic acid or alcohol until needed. This is not an efficient type of respiration. When oxygen is present, aerobic respiration occurs after glycolysis.

Both aerobic and anaerobic pathways oxidize glucose to pyruvate by glycolysis and both pathways have NAD$^+$ as the oxidizing agent. A substantial difference between the two pathways is that in fermentation an organic molecule such as pyruvate or acetaldehyde is the final electron acceptor. In respiration, the final electron acceptor is oxygen. Another key difference is that respiration yields much more energy from a sugar molecule than fermentation does. Respiration can produce up to 18 times more ATP than fermentation. However, respiration requires a ready supply of oxygen.

Competency 007   The teacher understands how specialized cells, tissues, organs, organ systems, and organisms grow and develop.

Analyze the role of stem cells in cellular differentiation

Differentiation is the developmental process in which undifferentiated (often embryonic) cells become specialized in structure and function. The fate of the cell is usually maintained through many subsequent generations. Gene regulatory proteins can generate many cell types during development by manipulating which genes are expressed in the cell and its subsequent lineage. Scientists believe that these proteins are passed down to the next generation of cells to ensure the specialized expression of the genes occurs.

Stem cells are not terminally differentiated. They can divide for as long as the animal is alive. When the stem cell divides, its daughter cells can either remain a stem cell or proceed with terminal differentiation. There are many types of stem cells that are specialized for different classes of terminally differentiated cells.

Embryonic stem cells give rise to all the tissues and cell types in the body. In culture, these cells have led to the creation of animal tissue that can replace damaged tissues. It is hopeful that with continued research, embryonic stem cells can be cultured to replace damaged muscles, tissues, and organs.

Animal tissue becomes specialized during development. For example in early development, the ectoderm (outer layer) becomes the epidermis or skin. The mesoderm (middle layer) becomes muscles and other organs beside the gut. The endoderm (inner layer) becomes the gut, also called the archenteron.

Understand the relationship between an unrestricted cell cycle and cancer

The restriction point, or the point at which the cell division cycle stops, occurs late in the G_1 phase. This is when the decision for the cell to divide is made. If all the internal and external cell systems are working properly, the cell proceeds to replicate. Cells may also decide not to proceed past the restriction point. This nondividing cell state is called the G_0 phase. Many specialized cells remain in this state. Cell division is discussed in more detail in the Mitosis section, below.

The density of cells also regulates cell division. Density-dependent inhibition is when the cells crowd one another and consume all the nutrients, therefore halting cell division. Cancer cells do not respond to density-dependent inhibition. They divide excessively and invade other tissues. As long as there are nutrients, cancer cells are "immortal" and continue to divide, forming tumors.

Recognize the levels of organization

Life is highly organized. The organization of living systems builds on levels from small to increasingly larger and more complex. Life is organized from simple to complex in the following general way:

Atoms-> molecules-> organelles->cells->tissues->organs-> organ systems-> organism

DOMAIN III.   HEREDITY AND EVOLUTION OF LIFE

Competency 008   The teacher understands the structures and functions of nucleic acids in the mechanisms of genetics.

DNA replication, potential errors, and implications of these errors

DNA replicates semi-conservatively. This means the two original strands are conserved with each strand serving as a template for a new strand. The two new DNA molecules are each composed of one original strand and one newly-synthesized strand.

In DNA replication, the first step is to separate the two strands. As they separate, the cell unwinds the supercoils to reduce tension. An enzyme called **helicase** unwinds the DNA as the replication fork proceeds and **topoisomerases** relieves the twisting tension by nicking one strand and relaxing the supercoil.

Once the strands have separated, they must be stabilized. Single-strand binding proteins (SSBs) bind to the single strands until the DNA is replicated.

An RNA polymerase called primase adds ribonucleotides to the DNA template to initiate DNA synthesis. This short RNA-DNA hybrid is called a **primer**. Once the DNA is single stranded, **DNA polymerases** add nucleotides in the 5' -> 3' (referring to the carbon positions within the sugar group) direction.

As DNA synthesis proceeds along the replication fork, it becomes obvious that replication is semi-discontinuous; meaning one strand is synthesized in the direction the replication fork is moving and the other is synthesized in the opposite direction ("backwards"). The continuously synthesized strand is the **leading strand** and the discontinuously synthesized strand is the **lagging strand**. As the replication fork proceeds, new primer is added to the lagging strand and it is synthesized discontinuously in small fragments called **Okazaki fragments**. These fragments are subsequently joined together into a single continuous strand.

The RNA primers that remain must be removed and replaced with deoxyribonucleotides. DNA polymerase has 5' -> 3' polymerase activity and has 3' -> 5' exonuclease activity. This enzyme binds to the nick between the Okazaki fragment and the RNA primer. It removes the primer and adds deoxyribonucleotides in the 5' -> 3' direction. The nick still remains until **DNA ligase** seals it producing the final product, a double-stranded segment of DNA.

Once the double-stranded segment is replicated, there is a proofreading system carried out by DNA replication enzymes. In eukaryotes, DNA polymerases have 3' -> 5' exonuclease activity—they move backwards and remove nucleotides where the enzyme recognizes an error, then add the correct nucleotide in the 5' -> 3' direction. In E. coli, DNA polymerase II synthesizes DNA during repair of DNA damage.

DNA Replication

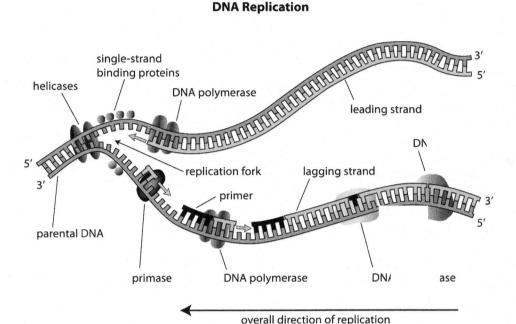

overall direction of replication

Protein synthesis

Proteins are synthesized through the processes of transcription and translation. Three major classes of RNA are needed to carry out these processes: messenger RNA (mRNA), ribosomal RNA (rRNA), and transfer RNA (tRNA). **Messenger RNA** contains information for translation. **Ribosomal RNA** is a structural component of the ribosome and **transfer RNA** carries ("transfers") amino acids to the ribosome for protein synthesis.

Transcription is similar in prokaryotes and eukaryotes. During transcription, one strand of the DNA molecule is copied into an RNA molecule (mRNA). Transcription occurs through the steps of initiation, elongation, and termination. Transcription also occurs for rRNA and tRNA, but the focus here is on mRNA.

Initiation begins at a region of DNA called the the promoter of the double-stranded DNA molecule. The promoter is a specific region of DNA that directs the **RNA polymerase** to bind to the DNA. The double-stranded DNA opens up and RNA polymerase begins transcription in the 5' -> 3' direction by pairing ribonucleotides to the deoxyribonucleotides as follows to get a complementary mRNA segment:

Deoxyribonucleotide		Ribonucleotide
A	->	U
T	->	A
G	->	C
C	->	G

Elongation is the synthesis on the mRNA strand in the 5' -> 3' direction. The new mRNA rapidly separates from the DNA template and the complementary DNA strands re-pair together.

Termination of transcription occurs at the end of a gene.
In eukaryotes, mRNA goes through **posttranscriptional processing** before going on to translation.

There are three basic steps of posttranscriptional processing:

1. **5' capping** – The addition of a methylated base protects the 5' end from degradation and serves as the site where ribosomes bind to the mRNA for translation.

2. **3' polyadenylation** – The addition of 100-300 adenines to the free 3' end of mRNA resulting in a poly-A-tail.

3. **Intron removal**- The removal of non-coding introns and the splicing together of coding exons to form the mature mRNA.

Translation is the process in which the mRNA sequence becomes a polypeptide. The mRNA sequence determines the amino acid sequence of a protein by following a pattern called the genetic code. The **genetic code** consists of 64 triplet nucleotide combinations called **codons**. Three codons are termination codons and the remaining 61 code for amino acids. There are 20 amino acids mRNA codes for and there is thus said to be redundancy in the genetic code because two or even three codons may code for the same amino acid. Amino acids are the building blocks of protein. They are attached together by peptide bonds to form a polypeptide chain.

Ribosomes are the site of translation. A ribosome is comprised of rRNA and proteins. Translation occurs in three steps: initiation, elongation, and termination. Initiation occurs when the methylated tRNA binds to the ribosome to form a complex. This complex then binds to the 5' cap of the mRNA. In elongation, tRNAs carry an amino acid to the ribosome and place it in order according to the mRNA sequence. Molecules of tRNA are very specific–they only accept one of the twenty amino acids that correspond to the anticodon. The anticodon is complementary to the codon. For example, using the codon sequence below:

the mRNA reads   A U G / G A G / C A U / G C U
the anticodons are   U A C / C U C / G U A / C G A

Termination occurs when the ribosome reaches any one of the three stop codons: UAA, UAG, or UGA. The newly formed polypeptide then undergoes posttranslational modification to alter or remove portions of the polypeptide.

Mutations in DNA molecules and their effect on protein structure and function

Inheritable changes in DNA are called mutations. **Mutations** may be errors in replication or a spontaneous rearrangement of one or more segments by factors like radioactivity, drugs, or chemicals. The severity of the change is not as critical as where the change occurs. DNA contains large segments of non-coding areas called introns. The important coding areas are called exons. If an error occurs on an intron, there generally is no effect. If the error occurs on an exon, it may be minor to lethal depending on the severity of the mistake. Mutations may occur on somatic or sex cells. Usually the mutations on sex cells are more dangerous since they contain the basis of all information for the developing offspring. But mutations are not always bad. They are the basis of evolution and if they create a favorable variation (very unlikely) that enhances the organism's survival they are beneficial. But mutations may also lead to abnormalities, birth defects, and even death. There are several types of mutations.

A **point mutation** is a mutation involving a single nucleotide or a few adjacent nucleotides. Let's suppose a normal sequence was as follows:

Normal sequence	A B C D E F
Duplication (a nucleotide is repeated)	A B C C D E F
Inversion (a segment is reversed)	A E D C B F
Insertion or **Translocation** (a segment of DNA is put in the wrong location)	A B C R S D E F
Breakage/Deletion (a segment is lost)	A B F (CDE lost)

Deletion and insertion mutations that shift the reading frame are **frame shift mutations**. They change the codon in which they occur but also potentially change all of the downstream codons as well because the cell always "reads" codons as triplets of base pairs.

A **silent mutation** does not change the amino acid sequence and therefore it does not alter the protein function. A **missense mutation** results in an alteration in the amino acid sequence. A mutation's effect on protein function depends on which amino acids are involved and how many are involved. The structure of a protein usually determines its function. A mutation that does not alter the structure will probably have little or no effect on the protein's function. However, a mutation that does alter the structure of a protein and can severely affect protein activity is called a **loss-of-function mutation**. Sickle-cell anemia and cystic fibrosis are examples of loss-of-function mutations.

Sickle-cell anemia is characterized by weakness, heart failure, joint and muscular impairment, fatigue, abdominal pain and dysfunction, impaired mental function, and eventual death. The mutation that causes this genetic disorder is a point mutation in the sixth amino acid of hemoglobin. A normal hemoglobin molecule has glutamic acid as the sixth amino acid and the sickle-cell hemoglobin has valine at the sixth position. This mutation causes the chemical properties of hemoglobin to change. The hemoglobin of a sickle-cell person has a lower affinity for oxygen, causing red blood cells to have a sickle shape under certain circumstances. The sickle shape of the red blood cell causes the formation of clogs because the cells do not pass through capillaries well.

Cystic fibrosis is the most common genetic disorder of people with European ancestry. This disorder affects the exocrine system. A fibrous cyst is formed on the pancreas that blocks the pancreatic ducts. This causes sweat glands to release high levels of salt. A thick mucous is secreted from mucous glands and accumulates in the lungs. This accumulation of mucous causes bacterial infections and possible death. Cystic fibrosis cannot be cured, but can be treated for a short while. Many children with the disorder die before adulthood. Scientists identified a protein that transports chloride ions across cell membranes. Those with cystic fibrosis have a mutation in the gene coding for the protein. The majority of the mutant alleles have a deletion of the three nucleotides coding for phenylalanine at position 508. Other people with the disorder have mutant alleles caused by substitution, deletion, and frameshift mutations.

Competency 009   The teacher understands the continuity and variations of traits from one generation to the next.

Identify the sequence of events in mitosis and meiosis and the significance of each process.

The purpose of cell division is to provide growth and repair in body (somatic) cells and to replenish or create sex cells for reproduction. There are two forms of cell division: mitosis and meiosis. **Mitosis** is the division of somatic cells and **meiosis** is the division of sex cells (eggs and sperm). The table below summarizes the major differences between the two processes.

Mitosis	Meiosis
1. Division of somatic cells	1. Division of sex cells
2. Two cells result from each division	2. Four cells (or polar bodies) result from each division
3. Chromosome number is identical to parent cell (diploid cells)	3. Chromosome number is half the number of parent cells (haploid cells)
4. Cell growth and tissue repair	4. Recombination provides genetic diversity during reproduction

Some terms to know:

gamete - sex cell or germ cell; eggs and sperm.

chromatin - loose chromosomes; this state is found when the cell is not dividing.

chromosome - tightly coiled, visible chromatin; this state is found when the cell is dividing.

homologues - chromosomes that contain the same information. They are of the same length and contain the same genes.

diploid - 2n number; diploid chromosomes are a pair of chromosomes (somatic cells).

haploid - 1n number; haploid chromosomes are a half of a pair (sex cells).

Mitosis

Mitosis is divided into two parts: the **mitotic (M) phase** and **interphase**. In the mitotic phase, mitosis and cytokinesis divide the nucleus and cytoplasm, respectively. This phase is the shortest phase of the cell cycle. Interphase is the stage where the cell grows and copies the chromosomes in preparation for the mitotic phase. Interphase occurs in three stages of growth: the **G1** (growth one) period, when the cell grows and metabolizes, the **S** (synthesis) period, when the cell makes new DNA, and the **G2** (growth two) period, when the cell makes new proteins and organelles in preparation for cell division.

The mitotic phase is a continuum of change, although we divide it into five distinct stages: prophase, prometaphase, metaphase, anaphase, and telophase.

During **prophase**, the cell proceeds through the following steps continuously, without stopping. First, the chromatin condenses to become visible chromosomes. Next, the nucleolus disappears and the nuclear membrane breaks apart. Then, mitotic spindles composed of microtubules form that will eventually pull the chromosomes apart. Finally, the cytoskeleton breaks down and the centrioles (if present) push the spindles to the poles, or opposite ends of the cell.

During **prometaphase**, the nuclear membrane fragments even more and allows the spindle microtubules to interact with the chromosomes. Kinetochore fibers attach to the chromosomes at the centromere region. **Metaphase** begins when the centrosomes are at opposite ends of the cell. The centromeres of all the chromosomes are aligned with one another along the metaphasic plane.

During **anaphase**, the centromeres split in half and homologous chromosomes separate. The chromosomes are pulled to the poles of the cell, with identical sets at either end. The last stage of mitosis is **telophase**. Here, two nuclei form with a full set of DNA that is identical to the parent cell. The nucleoli become visible and the nuclear membrane reassembles. A cell plate is seen in plant cells and a cleavage furrow forms in animal cells. The cell pinches into two cells. Finally, cytokinesis, or division of the cytoplasm and organelles, occurs.

Below is a diagram of mitosis.

Mitosis

Phase	Diagram	Description
Interphase	nucleus, chromosomes, centrioles	x number of chromosomes
Prophase	spindle fibers	chromosomes double (2x) and crossover
Prometaphase		nucleus dissolves and microtubules attach to centromeres
Metaphase		chromosomes align at middle of cell
Anaphase		separated chromosomes pull apart
Telophase		microtubules disappear cell division begins
Cytokinesis		2 cells formed each with x chromosomes

Meiosis

Meiosis is similar to mitosis, but there are two consecutive cell divisions, meiosis I and meiosis II in order to reduce the chromosome number by one half-the four resultant cells are haploid. This way, when the haploid sperm and haploid egg fuse during fertilization, the diploid number is reached.

Similar to mitosis, meiosis is preceded by an interphase during which the chromosomes replicate. The steps of meiosis I and meiosis II are as follows:

1. **Prophase I** – The replicated chromosomes condense and pair with homologues in a process called synapsis. This forms a tetrad. Crossing over, the exchange of genetic material between homologues to further increase diversity, occurs during prophase I.

2. **Metaphase I** – The homologous pairs attach to spindle fibers after lining up in the middle of the cell.

3. **Anaphase I** – The sister chromatids remain joined and move to the poles of the cell.

4. **Telophase I** – The homologous chromosome pairs continue to separate. Each pole now has a haploid chromosome set. Telophase I occurs simultaneously with cytokinesis. In animal cells, a cleavage furrow forms and, in plant cells, a cell plate appears.

5. **Prophase II** – A spindle apparatus forms and the chromosomes condense.

6. **Metaphase II** – Sister chromatids line up in the center of cell. The centromeres divide and the sister chromatids begin to separate.

7. **Anaphase II** – The separated chromosomes move to opposite ends of the cell.

8. **Telophase II** – Cytokinesis occurs, resulting in four haploid daughter cells.

The following is a diagram of meiosis.

Meiosis

Interphase		x number of chromosomes
Prophase		chromosomes double (2x) and crossover
Prometaphase		nucleus dissolves and microtubules attach to centromeres
Metaphase I		chromosomes align at middle of cell
Anaphase I		separated chromosomes pull apart
Telophase I		microtubules disappear cell division begins
Prophase II		2 cells formed each with x chromosomes
Metaphase II		microtubules attach to centromeres
Anaphase II		chromosomes pull apart
Telophase II		microtubules disappear cell division begins
Cytokinesis		4 cells form each with half the number of original chromosomes ($\frac{1}{2}x$)

Labels in diagram: nucleus, chromosomes, centrioles, spindle fibers

Identify the consequences of irregularities or interruptions of mitosis and meiosis

Please refer to the section entitled 'Mutations in DNA molecules and their effect on protein structure and function', above in Competency 008.

Apply principles of Mendelian genetics in working monohybrid and dihybrid crosses and crosses involving linked genes

Gregor Mendel is recognized as the father of genetics. His work in the late 1800's is the basis of our knowledge of genetics. Although unaware of the presence of DNA or genes, Mendel realized there were factors (now known as **genes**) that were transferred from parents to their offspring. Mendel worked with pea plants and fertilized the plants himself, keeping track of subsequent generations which led to the Mendelian laws of genetics. Mendel found that two "factors" governed each trait, one "factor" coming from each parent. Traits or characteristics came in several forms, known as **alleles**. For example, the trait of flower color had white alleles (*p*) and purple alleles (*P*). Mendel formulated two laws: the law of segregation and the law of independent assortment.

The **law of segregation** states that only one of the two possible alleles from each parent is passed on to the offspring. If the two alleles differ, then one is fully expressed in the organism's appearance (the dominant allele) and the other has no noticeable effect on appearance (the recessive allele). The two alleles for each trait segregate into different gametes. A Punnett square can be used to show the law of segregation. In a Punnett square, one parent's genes are put at the top of the box and the other parent's on the side. Genes combine in the squares just like numbers are added in addition tables. This Punnett square shows the *possible* results of the cross of two F_1 hybrids.

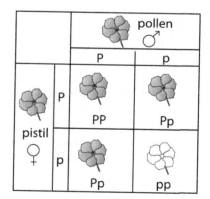

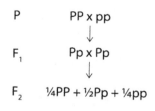

P   PP x pp

          ↓

F_1 Pp x Pp

          ↓

F_2 ¼PP + ½Pp + ¼pp

This cross results in a 1:2:1 ratio of F_2 offspring. Here, the *P* is the dominant allele and the *p* is the recessive allele. The F_1 cross produces three possible offspring with the dominant allele expressed (one *PP* and two *Pp*) and one possible offspring with the recessive allele expressed (one *pp*).

Some other important terms to know:

Homozygous – having a pair of identical alleles. For example, *PP* and *pp* are homozygous pairs.

Heterozygous – having two different alleles. For example, *Pp* is a heterozygous pair.

Phenotype – the organism's physical appearance.

Genotype – the organism's genetic makeup. For example, *PP* and *Pp* have the same phenotype (purple in color), but different genotypes.

The **law of independent assortment** states that alleles assort independently of each other. The law of segregation applies for monohybrid crosses (only one character, in this case flower color, is experimented with). In a dihybrid cross, two characters are explored. Two of the seven characters Mendel studied were seed shape and color. Yellow is the dominant seed color (*Y*) and green is the recessive color (*y*). The dominant seed shape is round (*R*) and the recessive shape is wrinkled (*r*). A cross between a plant with yellow round seeds (*YYRR*) and a plant with green wrinkled seeds (*yyrr*) produces an F_1 generation with the genotype *YyRr*. The production of F_2 offspring results in a 9:3:3:1 phenotypic ratio.

Based on Mendelian genetics, the more complex hereditary pattern of **dominance** was discovered. In Mendel's law of segregation, the F_1 generation has either purple or white flowers. This is an example of **complete dominance**. **Incomplete dominance** is when the heterozygous F_1 generation results in an appearance somewhere between the two parents. For example, red flowers are crossed with white flowers, resulting in an F_1 generation with pink flowers. The red and white traits are still carried by the F_1 generation, resulting in an F_2

generation with a phenotypic ratio of 1:2:1. In **codominance,** the genes may form new phenotypes. The ABO blood grouping is an example of codominance. A and B are of equal dominance (codominant) and O is recessive. Therefore, type A blood may have the genotypes of AA or AO, type B blood may have the genotypes of BB or BO, type AB blood has the genotype A and B, and type O blood has two recessive O genes.

Knowledge of pedigree charts

A family pedigree is a collection of a family's history for a particular trait. As you work your way through the pedigree of interest, the Mendelian inheritance theories are applied. In tracing a trait, the generations are mapped in a pedigree chart, similar to a family tree but with the alleles for the trait noted. In a case of simple Mendelian inheritance, where both parents have a particular trait and one of two children also expresses this trait, then the trait is due to a dominant allele. In contrast, if both parents do not express a trait and one of their children does, that trait is due to a recessive allele.

Analyzing genetic inheritance problems

The same techniques of pedigree analysis apply when tracing inherited disorders. Thousands of genetic disorders are the result of inheriting a recessive allele from both parents who likely are both heterozygous. These disorders range from non-lethal traits (such as albinism) to life-threatening (such as cystic fibrosis).

Most people with recessive disorders are born to parents with normal phenotypes. The mating of heterozygous parents would result in an offspring genotypic ratio of 1:2:1; thus 1 out of 4 offspring would express this recessive trait in their phenotype. The heterozygous parents are called carriers because they do not express the trait phenotypically but can pass the trait on to their offspring.

Lethal dominant alleles are much less common than lethal recessive alleles. This is because lethal dominant alleles are not masked in heterozygotes (i.e., there are no "carriers").

Mutations in a gene of the sperm or egg can result in a lethal dominant allele, usually killing the developing offspring.

Sex-linked traits - The Y chromosome found only in males (XY) carries very little genetic information, whereas the X chromosome found in males and females (XX) carries much important information. Since men have no second X chromosome to cover up a recessive gene, the recessive trait is expressed more often in men. Women need the recessive gene on both X chromosomes to show the trait. Examples of sex-linked traits include hemophilia and color-blindness.

These traits are called sex-linked because they appear far more frequently in men than women and thus their prevalence in the phenotype is linked to the sex of the individual.

Sex influenced traits - Traits are influenced by the sex hormones. Male pattern baldness is an example of a sex influenced trait. Testosterone influences the expression of the gene, thus, men are more susceptible to hair loss.

Nondisjunction - During meiosis, chromosomes may fail to separate properly. One sex cell may get both chromosomes and another may get none. Depending on the chromosomes involved this may or may not be lethal. Offspring end up with either a missing chromosome or an extra chromosome. An example of nondisjunction is Down Syndrome, where three copies chromosome 21 are present. Most nondisjunction events are lethal.

Chromosome Theory - Introduced by Walter Sutton in the early 1900's. In the late 1800's, the processes of mitosis and meiosis were understood. Sutton saw how this explanation confirmed Mendel's "factors". The chromosome theory basically states that genes are located on chromosomes that undergo independent assortment and segregation.

Analyze the techniques used to screen for genetic disorders

Some genetic disorders can be prevented. The parents can be screened for genetic disorders before the child is conceived or in the early stages of pregnancy. Genetic counselors determine the risk of producing offspring that may express a genetic disorder. The counselor reviews the family's pedigree and determines the frequency of a recessive allele. While genetic counseling is helpful for future parents, there is no certainty in the outcome. Additionally, if the mother will not accept abortion then post-conception genetic counseling is of dubious value.

There are some genetic disorders that can be discovered in a heterozygous parent. For example, sickle-cell anemia and cystic fibrosis alleles can be discovered in carriers by genetic testing (typically, this would be done only if the parents' families have a history of the genetic disease). If the parents are carriers but decide to have children anyway, fetal testing is available during the pregnancy. There are a few techniques available to determine if a developing fetus will have the genetic disorder.

Amniocentesis is a procedure in which a needle is inserted into the uterus to extract some of the amniotic fluid surrounding the fetus. Some disorders can be detected by chemicals in the fluid. Other disorders can be detected by karyotyping cells cultured from the fluid to identify certain chromosomal defects. Amniocentesis carries a small risk of miscarriage.

A physician removes some of the fetal tissue from the placenta in a technique called **chorionic villus sampling (CVS)**. The cells are then karyotyped as they are in amniocentesis. The advantage of CVS is that the cells can be karyotyped immediately, unlike in amniocentesis which take several weeks to culture. CVS carries a fairly high risk of miscarriage.

Unlike amniocentesis and CVS, **ultrasounds** are a non-invasive technique for detecting genetic disorders. Ultrasound can only detect physical abnormalities of the fetus.

Newborn screening is now routinely performed in the United States at birth. Phenylketonuria (PKU) is a recessively inherited disorder that does not allow children to properly break down the amino acid phenylalanine. This amino acid and its by-product accumulate in the blood to toxic levels, resulting in mental retardation. This can be prevented by screening at birth for this defect and treating it with a special diet.

Understand the role of nonnuclear inheritance

Mitochondrial DNA is passed to the next generation by the mother, via the mitochondria in the egg cell. A genetic defect in the mother's mitochondrial DNA will pass to her offspring, regardless of the paternal mitochondrial DNA.

Competency 010   The teacher understands the theory of biological evolution.

Analyze the conditions that affect the gene pool

Evolution currently is defined as a change in a population's genetic pool over time. Allele frequencies may shift and change from generation to generation. Populations evolve, individuals do not (and cannot) evolve. The **Hardy-Weinberg** theory of gene equilibrium is a simple mathematical prediction that models shifting gene patterns. Let's use the letter "*A*" to represent the dominant allele, and the letter "*a*" to represent the recessive allele. In a population, there are three possible genotypes: *AA, Aa* and *aa. AA* and *Aa* would have the dominant phenotype and only *aa* would have the recessive phenotype.

According to the Hardy-Weinberg theorem, there are five requirements that keep gene frequency stable and "prevent" evolution:

1. There is no mutation in the population.
2. There are no selection pressures; one allele is not beneficial over another allele in the environment.
3. There is no mating preference; mating is random.
4. The population is isolated; there is no immigration or emigration.
5. The population is very large (mathematical probability is more accurate with a larger sample).

The above conditions are impossible to meet in a real-world scenario. If these five conditions are not met, then gene frequencies will shift over time, leading to evolution. Let's say in a population, 75% of the population has the dominant phenotype (*AA* and *Aa*) and 25% have the recessive phenotype (*aa*). Using the following formula, we can determine the frequency of the *A* allele and the *a* allele in a population.

This formula can be used over generations to determine if evolution is occurring. The formula is: $1 = p^2 + 2pq + q^2$; where 1 is the total population, p^2 is the number of *AA* individuals, $2pq$ is the number of *Aa* individuals, and q^2 is the number of *aa* individuals.

Since you cannot tell by looking if an individual is *AA* or *Aa*, you must use the *aa* individuals to find that frequency first. As stated above *aa* was 25% of the population. Since $aa = q^2$, we can determine the value of q (or a) by finding the square root of 0.25, which is 0.5. Therefore, 0.5 (50%) of the alleles in the population are *a*. In order to find the value for p, use the following formula: $1 = p + q$. This would make the value of $p = 0.5$ (50%).

The gene pool is all the alleles of a given gene in all individuals of a population. The Hardy-Weinberg theorem describes infers that the frequencies of alleles in a population's gene pool are constant unless acted on by something other than sexual recombination.

Now, to find the number of *AA*, plug it into the first formula:

$$AA = p^2 = 0.5 \times 0.5 = 0.25$$
$$Aa = 2pq = 2(0.5 \times 0.5) = 0.5$$
$$aa = q^2 = 0.5 \times 0.5 = 0.25$$

Any test problem you may have with Hardy-Weinberg typically will be an obvious squared number. The square of that number will be the frequency of the recessive gene, and you can figure anything else out knowing the formula and the frequency of q.

When frequencies vary from generation to generation (that is, there is no Hardy-Weinberg equilibrium) the population is evolving. If the change to the gene pool is on a very small scale that it is called microevolution. Certain factors increase the chances of variability in a population, thus leading to evolution. Items that increase variability include mutations, sexual reproduction, immigration, large population size, non-random mating, and variation in geographic locale. Changes that decrease variation are natural selection, emigration, small population size, and random mating.

Recognize the relationship between phenotype and its selective advantage in the environment

The environment can have an impact on phenotype. For example, a person living at a higher altitude will have a different amount of red and white blood cells than a person living at sea level.

In some cases, a particular trait is advantageous to the organism in a particular environment. Sickle-cell disease causes a low oxygen level in the blood which results in red blood cells having a sickle shape. About one in every ten African-Americans have the sickle-cell trait. These heterozygous carriers are usually healthy compared to homozygous individuals who can suffer severe detrimental effects. In the tropical Africa environment, heterozygotes are more resistant to malaria than those who do not carry any copies of the sickle-cell gene. Thus, the environment determines fitness.

Sources of variation in a population

Heritable variation is responsible for the individuality of organisms. An individual's phenotype is based on inherited genotype and the surrounding environment.

Mutation and sexual recombination create genetic variation. **Mutations** may be errors in replication or spontaneous rearrangements of one or more segments of DNA. This topic is discussed above.

Mutations contribute a minimal amount of variation in a population. It is the unique **recombination** of existing alleles during sexual reproduction that causes the majority of genetic combinations in sexually reproducing species. Recombination is caused by the crossing over of the parent genes during meiosis. This results in unique offspring. With all the possible mating combinations in the world, it is obvious how sexual reproduction is the primary cause of genetic variation.

Analyze the role of natural selection on evolution

Natural selection is based on the survival of certain traits in a population through the course of time. The phrase "survival of the fittest," is often associated with natural selection. Fitness is the organism's ability to survive and thereby contribute to the gene pool of the population.

Natural selection acts on phenotypes. An organism's phenotype is constantly exposed to its environment. Based on an organism's phenotype, selection indirectly adapts a population to its environment by maintaining favorable genotypes in the gene pool.

There are three modes of natural selection. **Stabilizing selection** (very common) favors the more common phenotypes, **directional selection** (less common) shifts the frequency of phenotypes in one direction, and **diversifying selection** (fairly uncommon) favors individuals on both extremes of the phenotypic range.

Sexual selection leads to some of the secondary sex characteristics of males and females in a given species. Animals that use mating behaviors may be successful or unsuccessful. A male animal that lacks attractive plumage or has a weak mating call may not attract females, thereby eventually limiting that organism's genes in the gene pool.

Compare alternative mechanisms of evolution

There are two theories on the rate of evolution. **Gradualism** is the theory that minor evolutionary changes occur at a regular rate. Darwin's book, "On the Origin of Species," is based on this theory of gradualism. Huge changes therefore take a long period of time to occur as they are the gradual accumulation of numerous minor changes.

Charles Darwin was born in 1809 and spent 5 years in his twenties on a ship called the *Beagle*. Of all the locations the *Beagle* sailed to, it was the Galapagos

Islands that infatuated Darwin the most. There he collected thirteen species of finches that were quite similar. He could not accurately determine whether these finches were of the same species. He later learned these finches were in fact separate species. Darwin began to hypothesize that a new species arose from its ancestors by the gradual collection of adaptations to different environments. Darwin's most popular hypothesis involves the beak size of Galapagos finches. He theorized that the finches' beak sizes evolved to accommodate different food sources. Many people did not believe in Darwin's theories until recent field studies proved successful.

Although Darwin believed the origin of species was gradual, he was bewildered by the gaps in the fossil records of living organisms. **Punctuated equilibrium** is the model of evolution that states that organismal form diverges and new species form rapidly over relatively short periods of geological history, and then progress through long stages of stasis with little or no change. Punctuationalists use fossil records to support their claim. It is probable that both gradualism and punctuated equilibrium are correct, depending on the particular lineage studied.

Recognize the factors that lead to speciation

The most commonly used species concept in education is the **Biological Species Concept (BSC)** (note this concept has severe limitations as a practical methodology).

This concept states that a species is a reproductive community of populations that occupy a specific niche in nature. It focuses on reproductive isolation of populations as the primary criterion for recognition of species status (in other words, if two organisms can mate and have offspring they are the same species). The biological species concept does not apply to organisms that are asexual in their reproduction (most known species), fossil organisms (for obvious reasons), or distinctive populations that hybridize (e.g., horses and donkeys are not considered the same species even though they can produce mules and hinnies).

Reproductive isolation is caused by any factor that impedes two species from producing viable, fertile hybrids. Using the biological species concept, these reproductive isolation mechanisms will result in new species. Reproductive barriers can be categorized as **prezygotic** (before mating) or **postzygotic** (after mating).

Prezygotic barriers include:

1. Habitat isolation – species occupy different habitats in the same territory.
2. Temporal isolation – populations reaching sexual maturity/flowering at different times of the year.
3. Ethological isolation – behavioral differences that reduce or prevent Inter-breeding between individuals of different species (including pheromones and other attractants).
4. Mechanical isolation – structural differences that make gamete transfer difficult or impossible.
5. Gametic isolation – male and female gametes do not attract or bond with each other; no fertilization.

Postzygotic barriers include:

1. Hybrid inviability – hybrids die before sexual maturity.
2. Hybrid sterility – disrupts gamete formation; no normal sex cells.
3. Hybrid breakdown – reduces viability or fertility in progeny of the F_2 generation.

Geographical isolation can also lead to the origin of new species. **Allopatric speciation** is speciation without geographic overlap. It is the accumulation of genetic differences through division of a species' range, either through a physical barrier separating the population or through expansion by dispersal. In **sympatric speciation**, new species arise within the range of parent populations. Populations are sympatric if their geographical range overlaps. This usually involves the rapid accumulation of genetic differences (usually chromosomal rearrangements) that prevent inter-breeding with adjacent populations.

Competency 011   The teacher understands evidence for evolutionary change during Earth's history.

Knowledge of the theories of the origin of life

The hypothesis that life developed on Earth from nonliving materials is the most widely accepted theory. The transformation from nonliving materials to life is hypothesizes to have occurred in four stages. The first stage was the nonliving (abiotic) synthesis of small monomers such as amino acids and nucleotides (these processes can be reproduced in laboratory experiments). In the second stage, these monomers combine to form polymers, such as proteins and nucleic acids (these processes can be reproduced in laboratory experiments). The third stage was the accumulation of these polymers into droplets called protobionts (this process can be reproduced in the laboratory). The last stage was the origin of life and heredity, with RNA as the first genetic material.

The first stage of this theory was hypothesized in the 1920s. A. I. Oparin and J. B. S. Haldane were the first to theorize that the primitive atmosphere was a reducing atmosphere with no oxygen present. The gases were rich in hydrogen, methane, water, and ammonia. In the 1950s, Stanley Miller demonstrated Oparin's theory in the laboratory by combining the above gases. By using an electrical spark in the artificial environment, he was able to synthesize simple amino acids. It is commonly accepted that amino acids appeared before DNA. Other laboratory experiments have supported that the other stages in the origin of life theory could have happened.

Other scientists believe simpler hereditary systems originated before nucleic acids. In 1991, Julius Rebek was able to synthesize a simple organic molecule that replicates itself. According to his theory, this simple molecule may be the precursor of RNA.

Analyze the progression of life forms

Prokaryotes are the simplest life form. Their small genome size limits the number of genes that control metabolic activities. Over time, some prokaryotic groups became multicellular organisms for this reason. Prokaryotes then evolved to form complex bacterial communities where organisms benefit from one another.

The **endosymbiotic theory** of the origin of eukaryotes states that eukaryotes arose from symbiotic groups of prokaryotic cells. According to this theory, smaller prokaryotes lived within larger prokaryotic cells, eventually evolving into chloroplasts and mitochondria.

Chloroplasts are theorized to be the descendant of photosynthetic prokaryotes and mitochondria are theorized to be the descendants of bacteria that were aerobic heterotrophs. Serial endosymbiosis is a sequence of endosymbiotic events. Serial endosymbiosis may also play a role in the progression of life forms to become eukaryotes.

Understand the importance of geological and fossil records in determining evolution

Fossils are the key to understanding biological history. They are the preserved remnants left by an organism that lived in the past.   Scientists have established a generally accepted geological time scale to determine the age of a fossil. The geological time scale is broken down into four eras: the Precambrian, Paleozoic, Mesozoic, and Cenozoic. The eras are further broken down into periods that represent a distinct age in the history of the Earth and its life. Scientists use rock layers called strata to date fossils. The older layers of rock are at the bottom. This allows scientists to correlate the rock layers with the era they date back to. Radiometric dating is a more precise method of dating fossils. Rocks and fossils contain certain isotopes of elements at a different concentration than the environment in general. The isotope's half-life is used to date older fossils by determining the amount of isotope remaining and comparing it to the half-life.

Dating fossils is helpful in the construction of evolutionary trees. Scientists can arrange the succession of organisms based on their fossil record. The fossils of an organism's ancestors can be dated and placed on its evolutionary tree. For example, the branched evolution of horses shows that the modern horse's ancestors were smaller, had a higher number of toes, and had teeth modified for grazing.

DOMAIN IV.   DIVERSITY OF LIFE

Competency 012   The teacher understands similarities and differences between living organisms and how taxonomic systems are used to organize and interpret the diversity of life.

Knowledge of the classification of organisms

Scientists estimate that there are more than ten million different species of living things. Of these, 1.5 million have been named and classified. Systems of classification show similarities and assist scientists with a worldwide system of organization.

Carolus Linnaeus is considered the father of **taxonomy** (taxonomy is the science of classification). Linnaeus based his system on morphology (study of structure). Later on, evolutionary relationships (phylogeny) were also used to sort and group species. The modern classification system uses binomial nomenclature, a two-word name for every species. The genus is the first part of the name and the species is the second part. Notice in the levels explained below that *Homo sapiens* is the scientific name for humans (the genus and species, or generic and specific, name). Starting with the kingdom, the groups get smaller and more alike as one moves down the levels in the classification of humans:

Kingdom: Animalia, Phylum: Chordata, Subphylum: Vertebrata, Class: Mammalia, Order: Primate, Family: Hominidae, Genus: *Homo*, Species: *sapiens*

Several different morphological criteria are used to classify organisms:

1. **Ancestral characters** - characteristics that are unchanged over prolonged periods (e.g. 5 digits on the hand of an ape).

2. **Derived characters** - characteristics that have evolved more recently (e.g. the absence of a tail on an ape).

3. **Conservative characters** - traits that change slowly.

4. **Homologous characters** - characteristics with the same genetic basis but used for a different function. (e.g., wing of a bat, arm of a human. The bone structure is the same, but the limbs are used for different purposes).

5. **Analogous characters** – structures that differ, but used for similar purposes (e.g. the wing of a bird and the wing of a butterfly).

6. **Convergent evolution** - development of similar adaptations by organisms that are unrelated.

Biological characteristics are also used to classify organisms. Protein comparison and DNA comparison are powerful comparative methods used to measure evolutionary relationships between species. Taxonomists consider the organism's life history, biochemical (DNA) makeup, behavior, and geographical distribution. The fossil record is also used to show evolutionary relationships.

Analyzing a phylogenetic tree or cladogram of related species

The typical graphic product of a classification is a **phylogenetic tree**, which represents a hypothesis of the relationships of certain species based on branching of lineages through time within a group.

Every time you see a phylogenetic tree, you should be aware that it is making statements on the degree of similarity between organisms, or the particular pattern in which the various lineages diverged (phylogenetic history).

Cladistics is the study of phylogenetic relationships of organisms by analysis of shared, derived character states. Cladograms are constructed to show evolutionary pathways. Character states are polarized in cladistic analysis to be plesiomorphous (ancestral features), symplesiomorphous (shared ancestral features), apomorphous (derived features), and synapomorphous (shared, derived features). Cladistic analysis is a relatively new process.

Analyzing the impact of evolution and modern genetics in the classification system

The current five-kingdom system separates prokaryotes from eukaryotes. The prokaryotes belong to the Kingdom Monera while the eukaryotes belong to Kingdoms Protista, Plantae, Fungi, or Animalia. Recent comparisons of nucleic acids and proteins between different groups of organisms have led to problems concerning the five-kingdom system. Based on these comparisons, alternative kingdom systems have emerged. Six and eight kingdom systems as well as a three-domain system have been proposed as more accurate classification systems. It is important to note that classification systems evolve as more information regarding characteristics and evolutionary histories of organisms arise.

Competency 013   The teacher understands that, at all levels of nature, living systems are found within other living systems, each with its own boundaries and limits.

Identify the general characteristics of vertebrate and invertebrate development

Generally, animal tissue becomes specialized during development. Sponges are the simplest animals and lack true tissue. They exhibit no symmetry.

Diploblastic animals have only two germ layers: the ectoderm and endoderm. They have no true digestive system. Diploblastic animals include the Cnideria (jellyfish). They exhibit radial symmetry.

Triploblastic animals have all three germ layers. Triploblastic animals can be further divided into: Acoelomates, Pseudocoelomates, and Coelomates.

Acoelomates have no defined body cavity. An example is the flatworm (Platyhelminthe), which must absorb food from a host's digestive system.

Pseudocoelomates have a body cavity that is not lined by tissue from the mesoderm. An example is the roundworm (Nematoda).

Coelomates have a true fluid filled body cavity called a coelom derived from the mesoderm. Coelomates can further be divided into protostomes and deuterostomes. In the development of protostomes, the first opening becomes the mouth and the second opening becomes the anus. The mesoderm splits to form the coelom. In the development of deuterostomes, the mouth develops from the second opening and the anus from the first opening. The mesoderm hollows out to become the coelom. Protostomes include animals in the phyla Mollusca, Annelida, and Arthropoda. Deuterostomes include animals in phyla Ehinodermata and Vertebrata (including humans).

Development is defined as a change in form. Animals go through several stages of development after fertilization of the egg cell: cleavage, blastula, gastrulation, neuralation, and organogenesis.

Cleavage - the first divisions of the fertilized egg. Cleavage continues until the egg becomes a blastula.

Blastula - a hollow ball of undifferentiated cells.

Gastrulation - the time of tissue differentiation into the separate germ layers, the endoderm, mesoderm, and ectoderm.

Neuralation – early development of the basic nervous system components.

Organogenesis - the development of the various organs of the body.

Knowledge of physiological processes of animals

Animals constantly require oxygen for aerobic cellular respiration and need to remove carbon dioxide from their bodies. The respiratory surface must be large and moist to facilitate gas exchange. Different animal groups have different types of respiratory organs to perform gas exchange. Some animals use their entire outer skin for respiration (as in the case of worms). Fishes and other aquatic animals have gills for gas exchange. Ventilation increases the flow of water over the gills. This process brings oxygen and removes carbon dioxide through the gills. Fish use a large amount of energy to ventilate their gills. This is because the oxygen available in water is less than that available in the air. The arthropoda (insects) have tracheal tubes that send air to all parts of their bodies.

Gas exchange for smaller insects is provided by diffusion. Larger insects ventilate their bodies by a series of body movements that compress and expand the tracheal tubes. Vertebrates have lungs as their primary respiratory organ. The gas exchange system in all vertebrates is similar to that in humans, discussed in a later section.

Osmoregulation and excretion in many invertebrates involves tubular systems. The tubules branch throughout the body. Interstitial fluid enters these tubes and is collected into excretory ducts that empty into the external environment by openings in the body wall. Insects have excretory organs called Malpighian tubes. These organs pump water, salts, and nitrogenous waste into the tubules. These fluids then pass through the hindgut and out the rectum. Vertebrates have kidneys as the primary excretion organ. We describe this system in a later section.

Identify the structures and functions of the organs and systems of various kinds of animals

Skeletal System - The skeletal system functions in support and movement. Vertebrates have an endoskeleton, with muscles attached to bones. Skeletal proportions are controlled by area to volume relationships. Body size and shape is limited by the force of gravity.

Muscular System – The function of the muscular system is movement. There are three types of muscle tissue: skeletal, smooth, and cardiac. Skeletal muscle is voluntary. These muscles are attached to bones. Smooth muscle is involuntary, is found in organs, and enables functions such as digestion and respiration. Cardiac muscle is a specialized type of smooth muscle found in the heart.

Nervous System - The **neuron** is the basic unit of the nervous system. It consists of an axon, which carries impulses away from the cell body to the tip of the neuron; the dendrite, which carries impulses toward the cell body; and the cell body, which contains the nucleus. Synapses are spaces between neurons. Chemicals called neurotransmitters are found close to the synapse. The myelin sheath, composed of Schwann cells, covers the axon and provides electrical insulation.

Digestive System - The function of the digestive system is to break food down into nutrients and absorb it into the blood stream where it can be delivered to all cells of the body for use in cellular respiration. As animals evolved, digestive systems changed from simple absorption to a system with a separate mouth and anus.

Respiratory System - This system functions in the gas exchange of needed oxygen and carbon dioxide waste. It delivers oxygen to the bloodstream and picks up carbon dioxide for release out of the body. Simple animals diffuse gases from and to their environment. Gills allow aquatic animals to exchange gases in a fluid medium by removing dissolved oxygen from the water. Lungs maintain an optimal environment for gas exchange in terrestrial animals.

Circulatory System - The function of the circulatory system is to carry oxygenated blood and nutrients to all cells of the body and return carbon dioxide waste for expulsion from the lungs. Animals evolved from an open circulatory system to a closed system with vessels leading to and from the heart.

Identify the major steps of the physiological process in animals, such as respiration, reproduction, digestion and circulation

Animal respiration – takes in oxygen and gives off waste gases. For instance, a fish uses its gills to extract oxygen from the water. Respiration without oxygen is called anaerobic respiration. Anaerobic respiration in animal cells is also called lactic acid fermentation.

Animal reproduction – can be asexual or sexual. A variety of reproductive strategies are utilized. Some species lay eggs, some give live birth; others give live birth to incompletely developed offspring which mature in a special maternal body cavity. Rates of reproduction vary considerably among species.

Animal digestion – some animals only eat meat while others only eat plants. Many animals do both. Nature has created animals with structural adaptations appropriate to their diet. The purpose of digestion is to break down carbohydrates, fats, and proteins. Many organs are needed to digest food starting with the mouth.

Enzymes are catalysts that help speed up chemical reactions by lowering the energy of activation. Temperature, pH, and the amount of substrate all affect enzyme activity. Saliva is an enzyme that changes starches into sugars. Numerous enzymes are involved in digestion and metabolism.

Animal circulation – the blood temperature of all mammals stays relatively constant regardless of the outside temperature (within reason). Such temperature maintenance is the defining characteristic of endothermic ("warm-blooded") animals. On the other hand, the body temperature of exothermic ("cold-blooded") animals will vary with the environmental temperature.

Identify the structure and function of organs and systems of the human body

The function of the muscular system is to facilitate movement. There are three types of muscle tissue: skeletal, cardiac, and smooth.

Skeletal muscle is voluntary. These muscles are attached to bones and are responsible for their movement. Skeletal muscle consists of long fibers and is striated due to the repeating patterns of the myofilaments (made of the contractile proteins actin and myosin) that make up the fibers.

Cardiac muscle is found in the heart. Cardiac muscle is striated like skeletal muscle, but differs in the action potentialfrom skeletal muscles. Cardiac muscle is highly specialized.

Smooth muscle is involuntary. It is found near or in organs and enables functions such as digestion and respiration. Unlike skeletal and cardiac muscle, smooth muscle is not striated. Smooth muscle has less myosin and does not generate as much tension as the striated muscles.

The axial skeleton consists of the bones of the skull and vertebrae. The appendicular skeleton consists of the bones of the legs, arms and tail, and shoulder girdle. Bone is a connective tissue.

Parts of the bone include compact bone which gives strength, spongy bone which contains red marrow to make blood cells, yellow marrow in the center of long bones to store fat cells, and the periosteum, which is the protective covering on the outside of the bone.

In addition to bones and muscles, ligaments and tendons are important joint components. A joint is a place where two bones meet. Joints enable movement. Ligaments attach bone to bone. Tendons attach bone to muscle. There are three types of joints:

1. Ball and socket – allow for rotational movement. An example is the joint between the shoulder and the humerus. This joint allows the arms to move and rotate in many different ways.

2. Hinge – movement is restricted to flexion in a single plane. An example is the joint between the femur and the tibia (knee)

3. Pivot – allows for the complex flexion and rotation of the forearm at the elbow and the hands at the wrist.

Physiology of muscle contraction - The mechanism of skeletal muscle contraction involves a nerve impulse striking a muscle fiber. This causes calcium ions to flood the sarcomere (the contractile unit of a muscle fiber). The myosin fibers creep along the actin, causing the muscle to contract. Once the nerve impulse has passed, calcium is pumped out and the contraction ends.

Nervous System

The **central nervous system** (CNS) consists of the brain and spinal cord. The CNS is responsible for the body's response to environmental stimuli. The spinal cord is located inside the spine. It sends out motor commands for movement in response to stimuli. The brain is where responses to more complex stimuli occur. The meninges are the connective tissues that protect the CNS. The CNS contains fluid-filled spaces called ventricles. These ventricles are filled with cerebrospinal fluid which is formed in the brain. This fluid cushions the brain and circulates nutrients, white blood cells, and hormones.

The **peripheral nervous system (PNS)** consists of the nerves that connect the CNS to the rest of the body. The sensory division brings information to the CNS from sensory receptors and the motor division sends signals from the CNS to effector cells (generally, muscles). The motor division consists of the somatic nervous system and the autonomic nervous system. The somatic nervous system is controlled consciously in response to external stimuli. The autonomic nervous system is unconsciously controlled by the hypothalamus of the brain to regulate the internal environment. This system is responsible for the movement of smooth and cardiac muscles as well as the muscles used by other organ systems.

The **neuron** is the basic unit of the nervous system. It consists of a long axon, which carries impulses away from the cell body to the tip of the neuron; the dendrite, which carries impulses toward the cell body; and the cell body, which contains the nucleus. Synapses are spaces between neurons. Chemicals called neurotransmitters are found close to the synapse.

Nerve action depends on depolarization and an imbalance of electrical charges across the neuron's cell membrane. A polarized nerve has a positive charge outside the neuron. A depolarized nerve has a negative charge outside the neuron.

Neurotransmitters turn off the sodium pump, which results in depolarization of the membrane. This wave of depolarization (as it moves from neuron to neuron) carries an electrical impulse. This is actually a wave of opening and closing gates that allows for the flow of ions across the synapse. Neurons have an action potential--there is a threshold of the level of stimuli that must be met or exceeded in order for neuron to depolarize. This is called the "all or nothing" response.

Neurotransmitters are chemical messengers. The most common neurotransmitter is acetylcholine. Acetylcholine controls muscle contraction and heartbeat. A group of neurotransmitters, the catecholamines, include epinephrine and norepinephrine. Epinephrine (adrenaline) and norepinephrine are also hormones. They are produced in response to stress. They have profound effects on the cardiovascular and respiratory systems. These hormones/neurotransmitters can be used to increase the rate and stroke volume of the heart, thus increasing the rate of oxygen delivery through the blood to body cells.

Digestive System

The function of the digestive system is to break food down into nutrients and place them into the blood stream where they can be delivered to all the cells of the body for use in cellular respiration (metabolism).

The teeth and saliva begin digestion by breaking food down into smaller pieces and lubricating it so it can be swallowed. The lips, cheeks, and tongue form a bolus, or ball of food. It is carried down the pharynx by the process of peristalsis (wave-like contractions) and enters the stomach through a sphincter, which closes to keep food from going back up. In the stomach, pepsinogen and hydrochloric acid form pepsin, the enzyme that hydrolyzes proteins. The food is broken down further by this chemical action and is churned into acidic chyme. The pyloric sphincter muscle opens to allow the food to enter the small intestine.

Most nutrient absorption occurs in the small intestine. Its large surface area, resulting from its length and interior protrusions called villi and microvilli, allow for a great absorptive surface into the bloodstream. Chyme is neutralized with an infusion of bile to allow the enzymes found in the small intestine to function. Accessory organs function in the production of necessary enzymes and bile. The pancreas makes many enzymes to break down food in the small intestine. The liver makes bile, which breaks down and emulsifies fatty acids. Any materials left after the trip through the small intestine enters the large intestine. The large intestine functions to reabsorb water and produce vitamin K. The feces, or remaining waste, are passed out through the anus.

Accessory organs - although not part of the digestive tract, these organs function in the production of necessary enzymes and bile. The pancreas makes many enzymes to break down food in the small intestine. The liver makes bile which breaks down and emulsifies fatty acids

Respiratory System - The respiratory system functions in the gas exchange of oxygen and carbon dioxide waste. It delivers oxygen to the bloodstream and picks up carbon dioxide for release out of the body. Air enters the mouth and nose, where it is warmed, moistened, and filtered of dust and particles. Cilia in the trachea trap unwanted material in mucus, which can be expelled. The trachea splits into two bronchial tubes and the bronchial tubes divide into smaller and smaller bronchioles in the lungs. The internal surface of the lung is composed of alveoli, which are thin-walled air sacs. These allow for a large surface area for gas exchange. The alveoli are lined with capillaries. Oxygen diffuses into the bloodstream and carbon dioxide diffuses out of the capillaries to be exhaled out of the lungs. Hemoglobin, a protein, is the actual carrier of oxygen and carbon dioxide.

The thoracic cavity holds the lungs. The diaphragm muscle below the lungs is an adaptation that makes inhalation possible. As the volume of the thoracic cavity increases, the diaphragm muscle flattens out and inhalation occurs.

Circulatory System

The function of the closed circulatory system (**cardiovascular system**) is to carry oxygenated blood and nutrients to all cells of the body and return carbon dioxide waste to be expelled from the lungs. The heart, blood vessels, and blood make up the cardiovascular system.

The structure of the heart is shown below:

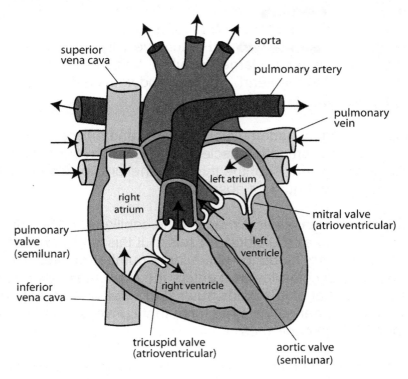

The atria are the chambers that receive blood returning to the heart and the ventricles are the chambers that pump blood out of the heart. There are four valves: two atrioventricular (AV) valves and two semilunar valves. The AV valves are located between each atrium and ventricle. The contraction of the ventricles closes the AV valve to keep blood from flowing back into the atria. The semilunar valves are located where the aorta leaves the left ventricle and the pulmonary artery leaves the right ventricle. The semilunar valves are opened by ventricular contraction to allow blood to be pumped out into the arteries and closed by the relaxation of the ventricles.

The cardiac output is the volume of blood per minute that the left ventricle pumps. This output depends on the heart rate and stroke volume. The **heart rate** is the number of times the heart beats per minute and the **stroke volume** is the amount of blood pumped by the left ventricle each time it contracts. Humans have an average cardiac output of about 5.25 L/min. Heavy exercise can increase cardiac output up to five times. Epinephrine and increased body temperature also increase heart rate and cardiac output.

Cardiac muscle can contract without any signal from the nervous system. It is the sinoatrial node that is the "pacemaker" of the heart. It is located on the wall of the right atrium and generates electrical impulses that make the cardiac muscle cells contract in unison. The atrioventricular node briefly delays the electrical impulse to ensure the atria empty before the ventricles contract.

There are three kinds of blood vessels in the circulatory system: arteries, capillaries, and veins. **Arteries** carry oxygenated blood away from the heart to organs in the body. Arteries branch off to form smaller arterioles in the organs. The arterioles form tiny **capillaries** that reach every tissue. At their downstream end, capillaries combine to form larger venules. Venules combine to form larger **veins** that return blood to the heart. Arteries and veins differ in the direction in which they carry blood.

Blood vessels are lined by endothelium. In veins and arteries, the endothelium is surrounded by a layer of smooth muscle and an outer layer of elastic connective tissue. Capillaries only consist of the thin endothelium layer and its basement membrane that allows for nutrient absorption.

Blood flow velocity decreases as it reaches the capillaries. The capillaries have the smallest diameter of all the blood vessels, but this is not why the velocity decreases. Arteries carry blood to such a large number of capillaries; the blood flow velocity actually decelerates as it enters the capillaries. Blood pressure is the hydrostatic force that blood exerts against the wall of a vessel. Blood pressure is greater in arteries. It is the force that conveys blood from the heart through the arteries and capillaries.

Blood is a connective tissue consisting of liquid plasma and several kinds of cells. Approximately 60% of the blood is plasma. It contains water, salts called electrolytes, nutrients, waste, and proteins. The electrolytes maintain a pH of about 7.4. The proteins contribute to blood viscosity and help maintain pH. Some of the proteins are immunoglobulins, the antibodies that help fend off infection. Another group of proteins are clotting factors.

Lymphatic System (Immune System)

The lymphatic system is responsible for returning lost fluid and proteins to the blood. Fluid enters lymph capillaries. This lymph fluid is filtered in the lymph nodes filled with white blood cells that fight off infection.

The two classes of cells in blood are red blood cells and white blood cells. **Red blood cells (erythrocytes)** are the most numerous. They contain hemoglobin, which carries oxygen.

White blood cells (leukocytes) are larger than red blood cells. They are phagocytic and can engulf invaders. White blood cells are not confined to the blood vessels and can enter the interstitial fluid between cells. There are five types of white blood cells: monocytes, neutrophils, basophils, eosinophils, and lymphocytes.

A third cellular element found in blood is platelets. **Platelets** are made in the bone marrow and assist in blood clotting. The neurotransmitter that initiates blood vessel constriction following an injury is called serotonin. A material called prothrombin is converted to thrombin with the help of thromboplastin. The thrombin is then used to convert fibrinogen to fibrin, which traps red blood cells to form a scab and stop blood flow.

The immune system is responsible for defending the body against foreign invaders. There are two defense mechanisms: non-specific and specific.

The **non-specific** immune mechanism has two lines of defenses. The first line of defense is comprised of the physical barriers of the body. These include the skin and mucous membranes. The skin prevents the penetration of bacteria and viruses as long as there are no abrasions on the skin. Mucous membranes form a protective barrier around the digestive, respiratory, and genitourinary tracts. In addition, the pH of the skin and mucous membranes inhibit the growth of many microbes. Mucous secretions (tears and saliva) wash away many microbes and also contain lysozyme that kills many microbes.

The second line of defense includes white blood cells and the inflammatory response. **Phagocytosis** is the ingestion of foreign particles. Neutrophils make up about seventy percent of all white blood cells. Monocytes mature to become macrophages which are the largest phagocytic cells.

Eosinophils are also phagocytic. Natural killer cells destroy the body's own infected cells instead of the invading the microbe directly.

The other second line of defense mechanism is the inflammatory response. The blood supply to the injured area is increased, causing redness and heat. Swelling also typically occurs with inflammation. Histamine is released by basophils and mast cells when the cells are injured. This triggers the inflammatory response.

The **specific** immune mechanism recognizes specific foreign material and responds by destroying the invader. These mechanisms are specific and diverse. They are able to recognize individual pathogens. An **antigen** is any foreign particle that elicits an immune response. An **antibody** is manufactured by the body and recognizes and latches onto antigens, hopefully destroying them. They also have recognition of foreign material versus the self. Memory of the invaders provides immunity upon further exposure (this is the basic mechanism of immunization).

Immunity is the body's ability to recognize and destroy an antigen before it causes harm. Active immunity develops after recovery from an infectious disease (e.g. chicken pox) or after a vaccination (e.g., mumps, measles, rubella). Passive immunity may be passed from one individual to another and is not permanent. A good example is the immunities passed from mother to nursing child. A baby's immune system is not well developed and the passive immunity they receive through nursing keeps them healthier.

There are two main responses made by the body after exposure to an antigen: humoral and cell-mediated.

1. **Humoral response** - Free antigens activate this response and B cells (lymphocytes from bone marrow) give rise to plasma cells that secrete antibodies and memory cells that will recognize future exposures to the same antigen. The antibodies defend against extracellular pathogens by binding to the antigen and making them an easy target for phagocytes to engulf and destroy. Antibodies are in a class of proteins called immunoglobulins. There are five major classes of immunoglobulins (Ig) involved in the humoral response: IgM, IgG, IgA, IgD, and IgE.

2. **Cell-mediated response** - Cells that have been infected activate T cells (lymphocytes from the thymus). These activated T cells defend against pathogens in the cells or cancer cells by binding to the infected cells and destroying them along with the antigen. T cell receptors on the T helper cells recognize antigens bound to the body's own cells. T helper cells release IL-2 which stimulates other lymphocytes (cytotoxic T cells and B cells). Cytotoxic T cells kill infected host cells by recognizing specific antigens.

Vaccines are antigens given in very small amounts. They stimulate both humoral and cell-mediated responses and help memory cells recognize future exposure to the antigen so antibodies can be produced much faster.

Endocrine System

The function of the **endocrine system** is to manufacture proteins called hormones. **Hormones** are released into the bloodstream and are carried to a target tissue where they stimulate an action. There are two classes of hormones: steroid and peptide. Steroid hormones come from cholesterol and include the sex hormones. Peptide hormones are derived from amino acids. Hormones are specific and fit receptors on the target tissue cell surface. The receptor activates an enzyme that converts ATP to cyclic AMP. Cyclic AMP (cAMP) is a second messenger from the cell membrane to the nucleus. The genes found in the nucleus turn on or off to cause a specific response.

Hormones are secreted by endocrine cells which make up endocrine glands. The major endocrine glands and their hormones are as follows:

Hypothalamus – located in the lower brain; signals the pituitary gland.

Pituitary gland – located at the base of the hypothalamus; releases growth hormones and antidiuretic hormone.

Thyroid gland – located on the trachea; releases calcitonin and thyroxine.

Gonads – located in the testes of the male and the ovaries of the female; testes release androgens and ovaries release estrogens and progesterone.

Pancreas – secretes insulin and glucagon.

Excretory System

The functional unit of the kidney is the nephron. The structures of the kidney and nephron are illustrated:

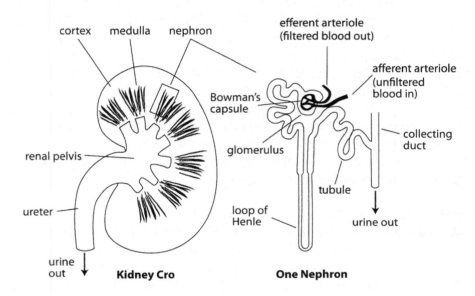

The Bowman's capsule contains the glomerulus, a tightly packed group of capillaries in the nephron. The glomerulus is under high pressure. Water, urea, salts, and other fluids leak out of the glomerulus and into the Bowman's capsule. This fluid waste (filtrate) passes through the three regions of the nephron: the proximal convoluted tubule, the loop of Henle, and the distal tubule. In the proximal convoluted tubule, unwanted molecules are secreted into the filtrate. In the loop of Henle, salt is actively pumped out of the tube and much water is lost due to the hyperosmosity of the inner part (medulla) of the kidney. As the fluid enters the distal tubule, more water is reabsorbed. Urine forms in the collecting duct that leads to the ureter then to the bladder where it is stored. Urine is passed from the bladder through the urethra. The amount of water reabsorbed back into the body is dependent upon how much water or fluids an individual has consumed. Urine can be very dilute or very concentrated depending on the level of concentration of waste.

Reproductive System

Hormones regulate sexual maturation in humans. Humans cannot reproduce until puberty, usually around the age of 8-14, depending on the individual. The hypothalamus begins secreting hormones that stimulate maturation of the reproductive system and development of the secondary sex characteristics. Reproductive maturity in girls occurs with their first menstruation and occurs in boys with the first ejaculation of viable sperm.

Hormones also regulate reproduction. In males, the primary sex hormones are the androgens (testosterone being the most important). The androgens are produced in the testes and are responsible for the primary and secondary sex characteristics of the male. Female hormone patterns are cyclic and complex. Most women have a reproductive cycle length of about 28 days. The menstrual cycle is specific to the changes in the uterus. The ovarian cycle results in ovulation and occurs in parallel with the menstrual cycle. This parallelism is regulated by hormones. Five hormones participate in this regulation, most notably estrogen and progesterone. Estrogen and progesterone play an important role in the signaling to the uterus and the development and maintenance of the endometrium. Estrogens are also responsible for the secondary sex characteristics of females.

Gametogenesis is the production of the sperm and egg cells. **Spermatogenesis** begins at puberty in the male. One spermatogonia, the diploid precursor of sperm, produces four sperm (refer to meiosis, above). The sperm mature in the seminiferous tubules located in the testes. **Oogenesis**, the production of egg cells (ova), is usually complete by the birth of a female. Egg cells are not released until menstruation begins at puberty. Meiosis forms one ovum with all the cytoplasm and three polar bodies that are reabsorbed by the body. The ovum are stored in the ovaries and released each month from puberty to menopause.

Sperm are stored in the seminiferous tubules in the testes where they mature. Mature sperm are found in the epididymis located on top of the testes. During ejaculation, the sperm travel up the **vas deferens** where they mix with semen made in the prostate and seminal vesicles and travel out the urethra.

Fertilization and embryogenesis

Ovulation releases the egg into the fallopian tubes that are ciliated to move the egg along. Fertilization of the egg by the sperm normally occurs in the fallopian tube. If pregnancy does not occur, the egg passes through the uterus and is expelled through the vagina during menstruation. Levels of progesterone and estrogen stimulate menstruation and are affected by the implantation of a fertilized egg so menstruation will not occur if the female is pregnant.

Identify the structures and functions of the parts of various types of plants.

Specialization of plant tissue enabled plants to get larger. Be familiar with the following tissues and their functions:

Xylem – transports water

Phloem – transports food (glucose)

Cortex – the outermost layer of a stem or root; storage of food and water

Epidermis – protection

Endodermis – controls movement between the cortex and the cell interior

Pericycle – meristematic tissue that can divide when necessary

Pith – storage in stems

Sclerenchyma and collenchyma – support in stems

Stomata – openings on the underside of leaves that let carbon dioxide in and water vapor out (transpiration)

Guard cells – control the size of the stomata (e.g. close stomata to conserve water)

Palisade mesophyll – contain chloroplasts in leaves and are the site of photosynthesis

Spongy mesophyll – open spaces in the leaf that allows for gas circulation

Seed coat – protective covering on a seed

Cotyledon – small seed leaf that emerges when the seed germinates

Endosperm – food supply in the seed

Apical meristem – an area of cell division allowing for growth

Flowers are the reproductive organs of the plant. Know the following functions and locations:

   Pedicel – supports the weight of the flower

Receptacle – holds the floral organs at the base of the flower

Sepals – green leaf-like parts that cover the flower prior to blooming

Petals – contain coloration by pigments to attract insects to assist in pollination

Anther – male part that produces pollen

Filament – supports the anther; the filament and anther make up the stamen

Stigma – female part that holds pollen grains produced by the anther
Style – tube that leads to the ovary (female)

Ovary – contains the ovules; the stigma, style, and ovary make up the carpel

Below is a diagram of a flower.

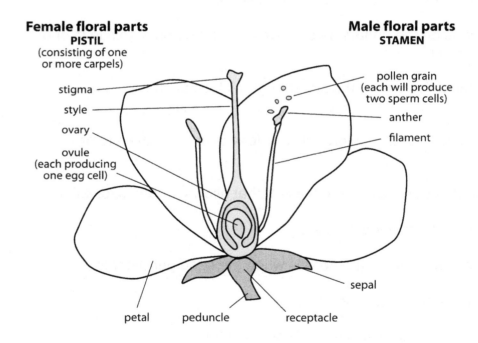

Competency 014   The teacher understands the processes by which organisms maintain homeostasis.

Analyze the processes involved in homeostasis

There are three homeostatic mechanisms; osmoregulation, excretion, and thermoregulation.

In animals, the kidneys are the site of osmoregulation. **Osmoregulation** deals with maintenance of the appropriate level of water and salts in body fluids for optimum cellular functions. The nephrons maintain osmoregulation by repeatedly filtering fluid waste and by reabsorbing excess water. Excretion is the elimination of metabolic (nitrogenous) waste from the body in the form of urea. The functional unit of excretion is the nephron, which make up the kidneys (the function of the nephron is described above).

Thermoregulation maintains the internal, or core, body temperature of the organism within a tolerable range for metabolic and cellular processes. Common indications of change in body temperature are shivering and sweating. Both are complex behaviors. The site for thermoregulation is the brain. It is the reception site for many hormones and therefore acts as a processing area. It integrates nerve impulses and commands activity. The heart functions to pump blood through the body, carrying life-sustaining nutrients to the cells.

Understand the feedback mechanisms in homeostasis

The thyroid gland produces hormones that help maintain heart rate, blood pressure, muscle tone, digestion, and reproductive functions. The parathyroid glands maintain the calcium level in blood and the pancreas maintains glucose homeostasis by secreting insulin and glucagon. The three gonadal steroids, androgen (testosterone), estrogen, and progesterone, regulate the development of the male and female reproductive organs.

Competency 015   The teacher understands the relationship between biology and behavior.

Analyze the importance of animal behaviors

Animal behavior is responsible for mating, communication between species, territoriality, aggression between animals, and dominance within a group. Animal communication is any behavior by one animal that affects the behavior of another animal. Animals use body language, sound, and smell to communicate. Perhaps the most common type of animal communication is the presentation or movement of distinctive body parts. Many species of animals reveal or conceal body parts to communicate with potential mates, predators, and prey. In addition, many species of animals communicate with sound. Examples of vocal communication include the mating "songs" of birds and frogs and warning cries of monkeys. Finally, many animals release scented chemicals to communicate with other animals. Pheromones are one class of scented chemicals that are important in reproduction and mating. Another class of distinctive odors, secreted from specialized glands, function to alert animals to the presence of others.

Innate behaviors are inborn or instinctual. An environmental stimulus such as the length of day or temperature may result in an innate behavior. Hibernation among some animals is an innate behavior. **Learned behavior** is modified due to past experience.

DOMAIN V. **INTERDEPENDENCE OF LIFE AND ENVIRONMENTAL SYSTEMS**

Competency 016 **The teacher understands the relationships between abiotic and biotic factors of terrestrial and aquatic ecosystems, habitats, and biomes, including the flow of matter and energy.**

Identify the major characteristics and processes of world biomes and communities, including succession, energy flow in food chains, and interrelationships of organisms

Ecology is the study of organisms, where they live, and their interactions with the environment. A **population** is a group of individuals of one species that live in the same general area. A **community** is a group of populations residing in the same area. Communities that are ecologically similar in regards to temperature, rainfall, and the species that live there are called **biomes**. The major terrestrial biomes are desert, grassland, tundra, boreal forest, tropical rainforest, and temperate forest.

Desert

Deserts exist at any location that receives less that 50 cm of precipitation a year. Despite their lack of water and often desolate appearance, the soils, though loose and silty, tend to be rich and specialized plants and animals do populate deserts. Plant species include xerophytes and succulents. Animals tend to be non-mammalian and small (e.g., lizards and snakes). Large animals are not able to find sufficient shade in the desert and mammals, in general, are not well adapted to storing water and withstanding heat. Deserts may be either hot and dry or cold. Hot and dry deserts are what we typically envision when we think of a desert, and they occur throughout the world. Hot deserts are located in northern Africa, the southwestern United States, and the Middle East. Cold deserts have similarly little vegetation and small animals and are located exclusively near the poles in Antarctica, Greenland, much of central Asia, and the Arctic. Both types of deserts do receive precipitation in the winter.

Grassland

As the name suggests, grasslands include large expanses of grass with only a few shrubs or trees. There are both tropical and temperate grasslands.

Tropical grasslands cover much of Australia, South America, and India. The weather is warm year-round with moderate rainfall. However, the rainfall is concentrated in half the year and drought and fires are common in the other half of the year. These fires serve to renew rather than destroy areas within tropical grasslands. This type of grassland supports a large variety of animals from insects to mammals both large and small such as squirrels, mice, gophers, giraffes, zebras, kangaroos, lions, and elephants.

Temperate grasslands receive even less rain than tropical grasslands and are found in South Africa, Eastern Europe, and the western United States. As in tropical grasslands, periods of draught and fire serve to renew the ecosystem. Differences in temperature also differentiate the temperate from the tropical grasslands. Temperate grasslands are cooler in general and experience even colder temperatures in winter. These grasslands support similar types of animals as the tropical grasslands: prairie dogs, deer, mice, coyotes, hawks, snakes, and foxes.

The savanna is grassland with scattered individual trees. Plants of the savanna include shrubs and grasses. Temperatures range from 0 - 25 degrees C in the savanna depending on its location. Rainfall is from 90 to 150 cm per year. The savanna is a transitional biome between the rain forest and the desert that is located in central South America, southern Africa, and parts of Australia.

Tundra

Tundra is treeless plain with extremely low temperatures (-28 to 15 degrees C) and little vegetation or precipitation. Rainfall is limited, ranging from 10 to 15 cm per year. A layer of permanently frozen subsoil, called permafrost, is found in the tundra. The permafrost means that no vegetation with deep root systems can exist in the tundra, but low shrubs, mosses, grasses, and lichen are able to survive. These plants grow low and close together to resist the cold temperature and strong winds. The few animals that live in the tundra are adapted to the cold winters (via layers of subcutaneous fat, hibernation, or migration) and raise their young quickly during the summers. Such species include lemmings, caribou, arctic squirrels and foxes, polar bears, mosquitoes, falcons, and snow birds.

Both arctic and alpine tundra exist, though their characteristics are extremely similar and are distinguished mainly by the location (arctic tundra is located near the North Pole, while alpine tundra is found in the world's highest mountains).

Forests

There are three types of forest, all characterized by the abundant growth of trees, but with differences in climate, flora, and fauna.

Boreal forest (taiga)

These forests are located throughout northern Europe, Asia, and North America, near the poles. The climate typically consists of short, rainy summers followed by long, cold winters with snow. The trees in boreal forests are adapted to the cold winters and are typically evergreens including pine, fir, and spruce. The trees form a canopy layer that is so thick that there is little undergrowth. A number of animals are adapted to life in the boreal forest, including many mammals such as bear, moose, wolves, chipmunks, weasels, mink, and deer. These coniferous forests have temperatures ranging from -24 to 22 degrees C. Rainfall is between 35 and 40 cm per year. This is the largest terrestrial biome.

Tropical rainforest

Tropical rainforests are located near the equator and are typically warm and wet throughout the entire year. The temperature is constant (25 degrees C) and the length of daylight is about 12 hours. The precipitation is frequent and occurs evenly throughout the year. In a tropical rainforest, rainfall exceeds 200 cm per year. Tropical rainforests have abundant, diverse species of plants and animals. A tropical dry forest gets scant rainfall and a tropical deciduous forest has wet and dry seasons. The soil is surprisingly nutrient-poor and most of the biomass is located within the trees themselves. The vegetation is highly diverse including many trees with shallow roots, orchids, vines, ferns, mosses, and palms. Animals are similarly plentiful and varied and include all type of birds, reptiles, bats, insects, and small- to medium-sized mammals.

Temperate forest

These forests have well defined winters and summers with precipitation throughout the year. Temperate forests are common in Western Europe, eastern North America, and parts of Asia. Common trees include deciduous species such as oak, beech, maple, and hickory. Unlike the boreal forests, the canopy in the temperate forest is not particularly heavy and so various smaller plants occupy the understory. Mammals and birds are the predominate forms of animal life. Typical species include squirrels, rabbits, skunks, deer, bobcats, and bear. The temperatures here range from -24 to 38 degrees C. Rainfall is between 65 and 150 cm per year.

A subtype of temperate forests are Chaparral forests. Chaparral forests experience mild, rainy winters and hot, dry summers. Trees do not grow as well here. Spiny shrubs dominate. Regions include the Mediterranean, the California coastline, and southwestern Australia.

Aquatic ecosystems

Aquatic ecosystems are, as the name suggests, ecosystems located within bodies of water. Aquatic biomes are divided between fresh water and marine. Freshwater ecosystems are closely linked to terrestrial biomes. Lakes, ponds, rivers, streams, and swamplands are examples of freshwater biomes. Marine areas cover 75% of the earth. This biome is further divided by the depth of the water. The intertidal zone is from the tide line to the edge of the water. The littoral zone is from the water's edge to the open sea. It includes coral reef habitats and is the most densely populated area of the marine biome. The open sea zone is divided into the epipelagic zone and the pelagic zone. The epipelagic zone receives more sunlight and has a larger number of species. The ocean floor is called the benthic zone and is populated with bottom feeders. Marine biomes include coral reefs, estuaries, and several systems within the oceans.

Oceans

Within the world's oceans, there are several separate zones, each with its own temperature profiles and unique species. These zones include intertidal, pelagic, benthic, and abyssal. The interdidal and pelagic zones are further distinguished by the latitude at which they occur (species have evolved to live in the various temperatures of water). The intertidal zone is the shore area, which is alternately under and above the water, depending on the tides. Algae, mollusks, snails, crabs, and seaweed are all found in the intertidal zones. The pelagic zone is further from land but near the surface of the ocean. This zone is sometimes called the euphotic zone. Temperatures are much cooler than in the intertidal zone and organisms in this zone include surface seaweeds, plankton, various fish, whales, and dolphins. Further below the ocean's surface is the benthic zone, which is even colder and darker. Much seaweed is found in this zone, as well as, bacteria, fungi, sponges, anemones, sea stars, and some fishes. Deeper still is the abyssal zone, which is the coldest and darkest area of the ocean and has high pressure and low oxygen content. Thermal vents found in the abyssal zone support chemosynthetic bacteria, which are in turn eaten by invertebrates and fishes.

Coral reefs

Coral reefs are located in warm, shallow water near large land masses. The best known example is the Great Barrier Reef off the coast of Australia. The coral itself is the predominant life form in the reefs and obtains its nutrients largely through photosynthesis. Many other animal life forms also populate coral reefs: many species of fish, octopuses, sea stars, and urchins.

Estuaries

Estuaries are found where fresh and seawater meet, for instance where rivers flow into the oceans. Many species have evolved to thrive in the unique salt concentrations (brackish water) that exist in estuaries. The species include marsh grasses, mangrove trees, oysters, crabs, and certain waterfowl.

Ponds and Lakes

As with the other aquatic biomes, many varied ecosystems occur in ponds and lakes. This is not surprising since lakes vary in size, depth, temperature, and location. Some lakes are even seasonal, lasting just a few months each year. Additionally, within lakes there are zones, comparable to those in oceans. The littoral zone, located near the shore and at the top of the lake, is the warmest and lightest zone. Organisms in this zone typically include aquatic plants and insects, snails, clams, fish, and amphibians. Further from land, but still at the surface of the lake is the limnetic zone.

Plankton is abundant in the limnetic zone and it is at the bottom of the food chain in this zone, ultimately supporting freshwater fish of all sizes. Deeper in the lake is the profundal zone, which is cooler and darker. Plankton also serves as a valuable food source in this zone since much of it dies and falls to the bottom of the lake.

Rivers and Streams

This biome includes moving bodies of water. As expected, the organisms found within streams vary according to latitude and geological features. Additionally, characteristics of the stream change as it flows from its headwaters to the sea. As the depth of rivers increases, zones similar to those seen in the ocean can be distinguished. That is, different species live in the upper, sunlit areas (e.g., algae, top feeding fish, and aquatic insects) and in the darker, bottom areas (e.g., catfish, carp, and microbes).

Wetlands

Wetlands are the only aquatic biome that is partially land-based. They are areas of standing water in which aquatic plants grow. These species, called hydrophytes are adapted to extremely humid and moist conditions and include lilies, cattails, sedges, cypress, and black spruce. Animal life in wetlands includes insects, amphibians, reptiles, many birds, and a few small mammals. Though wetlands are usually classified as a freshwater biome, they are often salt marshes that support shrimp, various fish, and grasses.

Succession is an orderly process of replacing a community that has been damaged or has previously not existed. Primary succession occurs where life never existed before, as in a flooded area or a new volcanic island. Secondary succession takes place in communities that were once flourishing but were disturbed by some source, either man or nature, but not totally stripped. A climax community is a community that is established and flourishing.

Definitions of feeding relationships:

There are many interactions that may occur between different species living together. Predation, parasitism, competition, commensalisms, and mutualism are the different types of relationships individuals in a population have with each other.

Predation and **parasitism** result in a benefit for one species and a detriment for the other. Predation is when a predator eats its prey. The common conception of predation is of a carnivore consuming other animals. This is one form of predation. Although not always resulting in the death of the plant, herbivory is a form of predation. Parasitism involves a predator that lives on or in its host, causing detrimental effects to the host. Many plants and animals have defenses against predators. Some plants have poisonous chemicals that will harm the predator if ingested and some animals are camouflaged so they are harder to detect.

Competition is when two or more species in a community use the same resources. Competition is usually detrimental to both populations. Competition is often difficult to find in nature because competition between two populations is not continuous. Either the weaker population will cease to exist, or one population will evolve to utilize other available resources.

Symbiosis is when two species live close together. Parasitism is one example of symbiosis. Another example of symbiosis is commensalism. **Commensalism** occurs when one species benefits from the other without harmful effects. **Mutualism** is when both species benefit from the other. Species involved in mutualistic relationships must co-evolve to survive. As one species evolves, the other must as well if it is to be successful in life. The grouper fish and a species of cleaner shrimp live in a mutualistic relationship. The shrimp feed off parasites living on the grouper. Thus, the shrimp are fed and the grouper stays healthy. Many microorganisms exist in mutualistic relationships.

Biogeochemical cycles are cycles important to life that involve both biotic and abiotic factors.

Water cycle - Two percent of all water is fixed in ice or the bodies of organisms. Available water includes surface water (e.g., lakes, oceans, rivers) and ground water (e.g., aquifers, wells). Ninety-six percent of all available fresh water is ground water. The water cycle is driven by solar energy. Water is recycled through the processes of evaporation and precipitation.

Carbon cycle - About .04% of the atmosphere is carbon dioxide gas. Plants fix carbon dioxide out of the atmosphere to produce glucose. Animals or decomposers eat the plants and are able to obtain carbon from the glucose. When animals release carbon dioxide through respiration, the plants again have a source of carbon for further fixation.

Nitrogen cycle - Seventy-eight percent of the atmosphere is nitrogen gas. Nitrogen must be fixed and taken out of the gaseous form to be incorporated into an organism. Only a few genera of bacteria have the correct enzymes to break the triple bond between nitrogen atoms in a process called nitrogen fixation. These bacteria live within the roots of legumes (e.g., peas, beans, alfalfa) and add nitrogen to the soil in organic molecules so it may be taken up by the plant. Nitrogen is necessary to make amino acids and the nitrogenous bases of DNA.

Phosphorus cycle - Phosphorus exists as a mineral and is not found in the atmosphere. Fungi and plant roots have structures called mycorrhizae that are able to fix insoluble phosphates into useable phosphorus. Urine and decayed matter return phosphorus to the earth where it can be fixed in the plant. Phosphorus is needed for the backbone of DNA and for ATP manufacturing.

Ecological Problems – Nonrenewable resources are fragile and we must conserve them for use in the future. Humankind's impact on the environment and willingness to conserve precious resources will control our future.

Biological magnification – Chemicals and pesticides accumulate along the food chain. Tertiary consumers have more accumulated toxins than animals at the bottom of the food chain.

Simplification of the food web - Three major crops feed the world (corn, wheat, and rice). The planting of these foods wipe out other habitats and push animals and plants from their native habitats into other habitats, often causing overpopulation or extinction.

Fuel sources – Strip mining and the overuse of oil reserves have depleted many resources. At the current rate of consumption, conservation or alternate fuel sources must be utilized.

Pollution – Although technology gives us many advances, pollution is a side effect of production. Waste disposal and the burning of fossil fuels have polluted our land, water, and air. Global warming and acid rain are two results of the burning of hydrocarbons and sulfur.

Global warming - rainforest depletion and the use of fossil fuels and aerosols have caused an increase in carbon dioxide production and destruction of ozone. As the ozone layer depletes, more heat enters our atmosphere and is trapped by greenhouse gasses (of which carbon dioxide is a significant component). This causes an overall warming effect which may eventually melt polar ice caps, causing a rise in water levels and changes in climate which will affect weather systems.

Endangered species - Many species are endangered, threatened, or have been driven to extinction by habitat destruction, over-hunting or over-fishing, or encroachment by humans.

Overpopulation - the human race is growing at a nearly exponential rate. The carrying capacity of our environment has not been exceeded due to our ability to use technology to produce more food and housing from limited resources. Space and water cannot be manufactured and eventually our overuse affects every living thing on the planet.

Competency 017 **The teacher understands the interdependence and interactions of living things in terrestrial and aquatic ecosystems.**

Flow of energy through trophic levels of an ecosystem

Trophic levels are based on the feeding relationships within an ecosystem; these relationships determine energy flow and chemical cycling.

Autotrophs are the primary producers of the ecosystem. **Producers** mainly consist of plants and photosynthetic protists and bacteria. **Primary consumers** are the next trophic level. The primary consumers are the herbivores that eat plants or algae. **Secondary consumers** are the carnivores that eat the primary consumers. **Tertiary consumers** eat the secondary consumer, etc. These trophic levels may go higher depending on the ecosystem. **Decomposers** are consumers that feed off animal waste and dead organisms. This pathway of food transfer is the food chain.

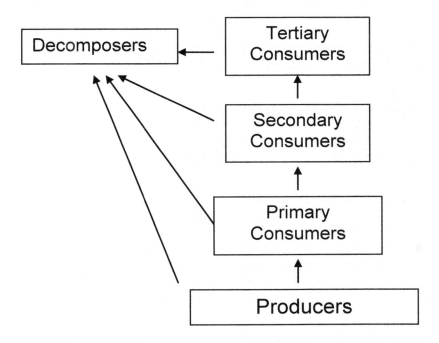

Most food chains are more elaborate, becoming food webs.

Pyramid models, Succession, and Abiotic and Biotic Factors

Energy is lost as the trophic levels progress from producer to tertiary consumer. The amount of energy that is transferred between trophic levels is called the ecological efficiency. The visual of this energy flow is represented in a **pyramid of productivity**.

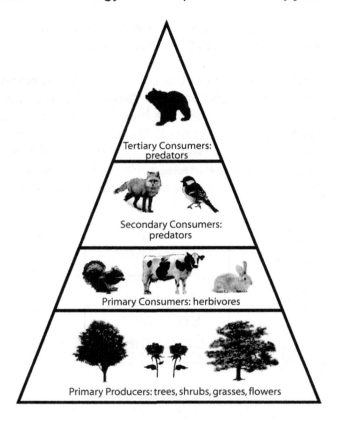

The **biomass pyramid,** shown above, represents the total dry weight of organisms in each trophic level. A **pyramid of numbers** is a representation of the population size of each trophic level. The producers, being the most populous, are on the bottom of this pyramid with the tertiary consumers on the top with the fewest numbers.

Succession is an orderly process of replacing a community that has been damaged or has begun where life previously did not exist. Primary succession occurs where life never existed before, as in a flooded area or a new volcanic island. Secondary succession takes place in communities that were once flourishing but were disturbed by some source, but not totally stripped. A climax community is a community that is established and flourishing.

Abiotic and biotic factors play a role in succession. **Biotic factors** are living things in an ecosystem (e.g., plants, animals, bacteria, and fungi). **Abiotic factors** are non-living aspects of an ecosystem (e.g., soil quality, rainfall, and temperature).

Abiotic factors affect succession by way of the species that colonize the area. Certain species will or will not survive depending on the weather, climate, or soil makeup. Biotic factors such as inhibition of one species due to another may occur. This may be due to some form of competition between the species.

Effects of biome degradation and destruction on biosphere stability

Humans are continuously searching for new places to form communities. This encroachment on the environment leads to the destruction of wildlife communities.

Conservationists focus on endangered species, but the primary focus should be on protecting the entire biome. If a biome becomes extinct, the wildlife dies or invades another biome.

Preservations established by the government aim at protecting small parts of biomes. While beneficial in the conservation of a few areas, the majority of the environment is still unprotected.

Competency 018   The teacher understands the relationship between carrying capacity and changes in populations and ecosystems.

Factors that affect population size and growth rate

A **population** is a group of individuals of one species that live in the same general area. Many factors can affect population size and population growth rate. Population size can depend on the total amount of life a habitat can support. This is the carrying capacity of the environment, an abstract concept of "how many" individuals of a given species could conceivably survive in that environment. Once the habitat runs out of available food, water, shelter, space, or some other critical factor, the carrying capacity has been met and more individuals will not be able to survive in that environment.

Limiting factors can affect population growth. As a population increases, the competition for resources is more intense, and the growth rate declines. This is a **density-dependent** growth factor. The carrying capacity can be determined by the density-dependent factor. **Density-independent factors** affect the individuals regardless of population size. The weather and climate are good examples. Too hot or too cold temperatures may kill many individuals from a population that has not reached its carrying capacity.

Population growth curves

A zero population growth rate occurs when the birth and death rates are equal in a population. Exponential growth occurs when there is an abundance of resources and the growth rate is at its maximum, called the intrinsic rate of increase. This relationship can be graphically represented in a growth curve, with time on the x-axis and the population size on the y-axis. An exponentially growing population begins with little change and then rapidly increases as seen in the J-curve below.

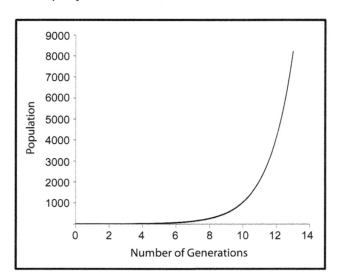

Logistic population growth incorporates the carrying capacity into the growth rate by using a relatively simple mathematical formula. As a population reaches the carrying capacity, the growth rate begins to slow down and level off as depicted in the S-curve below.

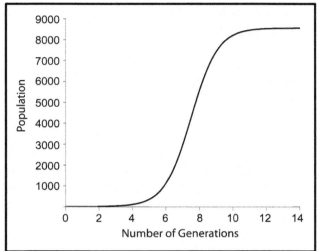

Many populations follow this model of population growth. Humans, however, currently are an exponentially growing population. Eventually, the carrying capacity of the Earth will be reached, and the growth rate will level off.

Relationships among organisms in a community

There are many interactions that may occur between different species living together. Predation, parasitism, competition, commensalism, and mutualism are the different types of relationships populations have amongst each other (these are described above).

Effects of population density on the environment

Population density is the number of individuals per unit area or volume. The spacing pattern of individuals in an area is dispersion. **Dispersion patterns** can be clumped, with individuals grouped in patches; uniform, where individuals are approximately equidistant from each other; or random.

Population densities are usually estimated based on a few representative plots. Aggregation of a population in a relatively small geographic area can have detrimental effects to the environment. Food, water, and other resources will be rapidly consumed, resulting in an unstable environment. A low population density generally is less harmful to the environment. The use of natural resources will be more widespread, allowing for the environment to recover and continue growth.

DOMAIN VI.   SCIENCE LEARNING, INSTRUCTION AND ASSESSMENT

Competency 019   The teacher understands research-based theoretical and practical knowledge about teaching science, how students learn science, and the role of scientific inquiry in science instruction.

Science is a body of knowledge systematically derived from study, observation, and experimentation. Its goal is to identify and establish principles and theories that may be applied to solve problems.

It is easiest for people to learn things that make senses to them. Individuals have preferred learning styles. Some prefer reading, others lecture, some visual representation, and some prefer hands-on experiments. It is important that teachers include different types of activities in their lessons to accommodate students of all styles of learning. It also helps to draw on everyday experience, relating science to the lives of the students.

Biological science, technology, and other sciences are closely connected and they all have tremendous impact on society and everyday life. Scientific discoveries often lead to technological advances and, conversely, technology is often necessary for scientific investigation. Advances in technology often expand the reach of scientific discoveries. In addition, biology and the other scientific disciplines share several unifying concepts and processes that help unify the study of science.

Because biology is the study of living things, we can easily apply the knowledge of biology to daily life and personal decision-making. For example, biological knowledge greatly influences the health decisions humans make every day. What foods to eat, when and how to exercise, and how often to bathe are just a few of the many decisions we make every day that are based, in part, on our knowledge of biology. Other areas of daily life where biological knowledge may affect decision-making are parenting, interpersonal relationships, family planning, and consumer spending.

An inquiring mind is at the heart of the scientific method. Teachers should encourage thought by asking open-ended questions. Science is not merely about creating; it is also about assessment and solutions. We can think of science as a loop. One questions something, and creates an experiment to study it. One can learn from this evidence, and then ask more questions. In-depth learning involves looking at the experimental data from all angles and continuing to seek knowledge. Learning in depth does not occur by looking at something superficially or by taking someone else's data as "proof".

Science is a self-correcting process that eventually identifies misconceptions and experimental biases. The scientific process encourages periodic reassessment. The conclusion step of the scientific method allows one to examine the hypothesis as it relates to their experimental data. At this point, one can find positive correlations or discord. When results are unexpected, one should revisit all possible sources of error. If an error is not found to explain the results, one can reconsider the hypothesis and also think about other possibilities. This is why experimentation often results in further experimentation.

Competency 020 **The teacher knows how to monitor and assess science learning in laboratory, field, and classroom settings.**

Some of the field techniques described here are site selection, field procedures, sampling, capture/recapture, transects, collecting techniques, and environmental assessment. We will look at each of these individually.

Site selection

Site selection in any field experiment is a critical factor. It depends on a number of issues including the type of research, the duration of the investigation, the accessibility of the site to a city/town, and transportation to the site. A group of researchers from the research team determine the selection of a site by studying all of the site aspects. They then make their recommendations and the research team collectively approves the site. If the first choice is found to be unsuitable a second, more suitable site will be selected. Most importantly, all the researchers must be reasonably comfortable with the site.

Field procedures

Proper field procedures ensure successful sample collection.

These include:

1. Preparing for field study (identifying learning objectives and the purpose of the field study)
2. Site selection
3. Sample collection
4. Preserving collected specimens

Sampling

Sampling involves the collection of pieces/specimens or the making of observations at determined intervals or areas for the purpose of research and investigation. Sampling includes animal tracking, capturing, plant and animal tagging, plot sampling, specimen collecting, transect sampling, and water sampling. Researchers use the results as representative of the whole research area or population. If improper sampling is performed the experimental results will be worthless.

Capture/recapture

Capture/recapture are methods commonly used in ecological studies. These methods are also known as mark/capture, capture-mark-recapture, sight-resight, and band recovery.

A researcher visits the study area (see site selection) and uses traps to capture live organisms. He or she marks each of these with a unique identifier – for example, a numbered tag/band – and then releases the organism unharmed back into the environment. Next, the researcher returns and captures another sample set of organisms.

Some of the organisms in the second sample will have been marked during the first visit and are known as recaptures. The unmarked organisms are tagged just like the previous ones. Scientists can estimate population from as few as two visits to the study area, but usually they make more than two visits. Migratory waterfowl often are banded with instructions to hunters to contact the study agency if they happen to shoot the marked bird.

Transect

A transect is a path along which a scientist records and/or counts occurrences of the phenomenon of study (e.g., a species of tree, for instance, by noting each individual plant's distance from the path). At the same time, obtain the distance of the object from the path. This results in an estimate of the area covered. Using transect results one can estimate the actual density of the studied organism.

Collecting techniques

The objective of capturing an animal is to identify it. There are six steps involved in this seemingly simple procedure of collecting insect specimen:

1. Catching – It is very difficult to catch insects like butterflies and dragon flies since they are very quick and the person trying to catch them must be quicker. The easiest method involves the use of a net.

2. Enveloping – Involves placing the insect wings folded in a glassine envelope, labeling it, and numbering it. This way, when the scientist opens the bag at a later date, the information needed is on the envelope.

3. Acetoning – After leaving the specimen for several hours (in this time the specimen will empty its intestines), one sacrifices the specimen by immersing it briefly in acetone. The scientist then straightens the insect and returns it to acetone and leaves it there for 16-24 hours. Acetone extracts water and fat from the specimen causing it to dry.

4. Removing – Removing the specimen from acetone and allowing the specimens to dry in a location away from people, since acetone fumes are harmful to humans.

5. Labeling – All the pertinent information must be attached to the specimen so the information is clear at a later date when someone else is studying the specimen.

6. Storing – The preserved specimen must be stored in a box protected from humidity and pests.

Environmental quality assessment

Environmental assessment involves collecting information, analyzing it using scientific principles, and evaluating the quality and conditions of the type of environment under study (e.g., marine, coastal, lake, etc.). Environmental assessment is absolutely essential to determine the hazards that are causing pollution and their effect on human and other life forms. The environmental quality assessment is done on a site or collection of sites, for a short period of time or for a number of years. Whatever may be the size of the test site or the duration of the investigation, the basic aim is to determine the quality of that particular environment. Some environmental projects study water quality, air quality, sediment and soil assessment, ground water assessment, and oil spills and their effect on marine life. Federal and State organizations generally monitor water and air quality on a regular basis.

Sample Essays

1. Using your accumulated knowledge, discuss the components of biogeochemical cycles.

Best Response:

Essential elements are recycled through an ecosystem. At times, the element needs to be made available in a useable form. Cycles are dependent on plants, algae, and bacteria to fix nutrients for use by animals. The four main cycles are: water, carbon, nitrogen, and phosphorous.

Water is recycled through the processes of evaporation and precipitation. Most living things require a ready supply of water, either fresh water or, using special adaptations, salt water.
 Plants fix carbon from the atmosphere in the form of carbon dioxide into the form of glucose. Animals eat the plants and are able to obtain the carbon necessary to sustain themselves. When animals release carbon dioxide through respiration, the cycle begins again as plants recycle the carbon through photosynthesis.

Most of the atmosphere is nitrogen gas. Nitrogen must be fixed and taken out of the gaseous form to be incorporated into an organism. Only a few genera of bacteria have the correct enzymes to break the strong triple bond between nitrogen atoms. These special bacteria live within the roots of legumes and fix nitrogen into organic compounds which are then taken-up by the plant. Nitrogen is necessary in the building of amino acids and the nitrogenous bases of DNA.

Phosphorus exists as a mineral and is not found in the atmosphere. Fungi and plant roots have structures called mycorrhizae that are able to fix insoluble phosphates into useable phosphorus. Urine and decayed matter returns phosphorus to the earth where it can be fixed in the plant. Phosphorus is needed for the backbone of DNA and for the manufacture of ATP.

The four biogeochemical cycles operate concurrently. Water is continually recycled, and is utilized by organisms to sustain life. Carbon is also a necessary component for life. Water, carbon, and nitrogen can be found in the air and on the ground. Phosphorous is commonly found in the ground. Special organisms, called decomposers, help to make these elements available in the environment once they have been utilized by once-living organisms. Plants use the recycled materials for energy and, when these plants are consumed, the cycle begins again.

Better Response:

Essential elements are recycled through an ecosystem. Cycles are dependent on plants, algae, and bacteria to make nutrients available for use by animals. The four main cycles are: water, carbon, nitrogen, and phosphorous. Water is typically available as surface water (large bodies of water) or ground water. Water is recycled through the states of gas, liquid (rain), and solid (ice or snow). Carbon is necessary for life as it is the basis for organic matter. Carbon dioxide from the atmosphere is fixed into organic glucose during photosynthesis. Nitrogen is the largest component of the atmosphere. It is also necessary for the creation of amino acids and the nitrogenous bases of DNA. Phosphorous is another elemental cycle. Phosphorous is found in the soil and is used in the manufacture of DNA and ATP.

Basic Response:

Elements are recycled through an ecosystem. This occurs through cycles. These important cycles are called biogeochemical cycles. The water cycle consists of water moving from bodies of water into the air and back again as precipitation. The carbon cycle includes all organisms, for example mammals breathe out carbon dioxide and are partially made of carbon molecules. Nitrogen is an amino acid building block and is found in soil. As things are broken down, phosphorous is added to the earth, enriching the soil, from where it taken up by bacteria.

2. Examine the components of a eukaryotic cell.

Best Response:

The cell is the basic unit of all living things. Eukaryotic cells are found in protists, fungi, plants, and animals. Eukaryotic cells are highly organized by internal membranes. They contain many organelles, which are membrane bound areas for specific functions. Their cytoplasm contains a cytoskeleton that provides a protein framework for the cell. The cytoplasm also supports the organelles and contains the ions and molecules necessary for cell function. The cytoplasm is contained by the plasma membrane. The plasma membrane allows molecules to pass in and out of the cell. The membrane can bud inward to engulf outside material in a process called endocytosis. Exocytosis is a secretory mechanism, the reverse of endocytosis.

Eukaryotes have a nucleus. The nucleus is the "brain" of the cell that contains all of the cell's genetic information. The genetic information is contained on chromosomes that consist of chromatin, which are complexes of DNA and proteins. The chromosomes are tightly coiled to conserve space while providing a large surface area. The nucleus is the site of transcription of the DNA into RNA. The nucleolus is where ribosomes are made. There is at least one of these dark-staining bodies inside the nucleus of most eukaryotes.

The nuclear envelope is two membranes separated by a narrow space. The envelope contains many pores that let RNA and ribosomes out of the nucleus.

Ribosomes are the site for protein synthesis. They may be free floating in the cytoplasm or attached to the endoplasmic reticulum. There may be up to a half a million ribosomes in a cell, depending on how much protein the cell makes.

The endoplasmic reticulum (ER) is folded membrane and provides a large surface area. It is the "roadway" of the cell and allows for transport of materials through and out of the cell. There are two types of ER: smooth and rough. Smooth endoplasmic reticulum contains no ribosomes on the surface. This is the site of lipid synthesis. Rough endoplasmic reticulum has ribosomes on its surfaces. It aids in the synthesis of proteins that are destined for secretion or otherwise need to be contained within a membrane.

Many of the products made in the ER proceed to the Golgi apparatus. The Golgi apparatus functions to sort, modify, and package molecules that are made in the other parts of the cell. These molecules are either sent out of the cell or to other organelles within the cell. The Golgi apparatus is a stacked structure to increase the surface area.

Lysosomes are found mainly in animal cells. These contain digestive enzymes that break down food, unnecessary substances, viruses, damaged cell components, and eventually the cell itself.

Mitochondria are large organelles that are the site of cellular respiration, where ATP is made to supply energy to the cell. Muscle cells have many mitochondria because they use a great deal of energy. Mitochondria have their own DNA, RNA, and ribosomes and are capable of reproducing by binary fission if there is a great demand for additional energy. Mitochondria have two membranes: a smooth outer membrane and a folded inner membrane. The folds inside the mitochondria are called cristae. They provide a large surface area for cellular respiration to occur.

Plastids are found only in photosynthetic organisms. They are similar to the mitochondira due to the double membrane structure. They also have their own DNA, RNA, and ribosomes and can reproduce if the need for the increased capture of sunlight becomes necessary. There are several types of plastids. Chloroplasts are the sight of photosynthesis.

Found in plant cells only, the cell wall is composed of cellulose and fibers. It is thick enough for support and protection, yet porous enough to allow water and dissolved substances to enter. Vacuoles are found mostly in plant cells. They hold stored food and pigments. Their large size allows them to fill with water in order to provide turgor pressure. Lack of turgor pressure causes a plant to wilt.

The cytoskeleton, found in both animal and plant cells, is composed of protein filaments attached to the plasma membrane and organelles. They provide a framework for the cell and aid in cell movement. They constantly change shape and move about. Three types of fibers make up the cytoskeleton.

Better Response:

The cell is the basic unit of all living things. Eukaryotic cells are found in protists, fungi, plants, and animals. Eukaryotic cells are organized. Their cytoplasm contains a cytoskeleton that provides a protein framework for the cell. The cytoplasm is contained by the plasma membrane. The plasma membrane allows molecules to pass in and out of the cell.

Eukaryotes have a nucleus. The nucleus is the "brain" of the cell that contains all of the cell's genetic information. The chromosomes house genetic information and are tightly coiled to conserve space while providing a large surface area. The nucleus is the site of transcription of the DNA into RNA. The nucleolus is where ribosomes are made.

Ribosomes are the site for protein synthesis. There may be up to a half a million ribosomes in a cell, depending on how much protein is made by the cell.

The endoplasmic reticulum (ER) is folded and provides a large surface area. It is the "roadway" of the cell and allows for transport of materials through and out of the cell. It may be smooth or rough.

Many of the products made in the ER proceed to the Golgi apparatus. The Golgi apparatus functions to sort, modify, and package molecules that are made in the other parts of the cell.

Mitochondria are large organelles that are the site of cellular respiration, where ATP is made to supply energy to the cell. Mitochondria have their own DNA, RNA, and ribosomes and are capable of reproducing by binary fission if there is a greater demand for additional energy.

Plastids are found only in photosynthetic organisms. They are similar to the mitochondria. They also have their own DNA, RNA, and ribosomes and can reproduce if the need for the increased capture of sunlight becomes necessary.

Found in plant cells only, the cell wall is composed of cellulose and fibers. It is thick enough for support and protection, yet porous enough to allow water and dissolved substances to enter.

Basic Response:

The cell is the basic unit of all living things. Eukaryotic cells contain many organelles. Eukaryotes have a nucleus. The nucleus is the "brain" of the cell that contains all of the cell's genetic information. The nucleus is the site of DNA transcription. There is at least one nucleolus inside the nucleus of most eukaryotes. Ribosomes are the site for protein synthesis and can be found on the rough endoplasmic reticulum (ER) and in the cytoplasm. The Golgi apparatus functions to sort, modify, and package molecules that are made in the other parts of the cell. Mitochondria are large organelles that are the site of cellular respiration, where ATP is made to supply energy to the cell.

In plant cells, the cell wall is composed of cellulose and fibers. The cytoskeleton, found in both animal and plant cells, is composed of protein filaments. The three types of fibers differ in size and help the cell to keep its shape and aid in movement.

3. Discuss the scientific process.

Best Response:

Science is a body of knowledge that is systematically derived from study, observations, and experimentation. Its goal is to identify and establish principles and theories that may be applied to solve problems.
Scientific experimentation must be repeatable. Experimentation leads to theories that can be disproved and are changeable. Science depends on communication, agreement, and disagreement among scientists. It is composed of theories, laws, and hypotheses.

A hypothesis is an unproved theory or educated guess followed by research to best explain a phenomenon. A theory is a hypothesis with supporting experimentation.

A theory is the formation of principles or relationships that have been verified and accepted.

A law is an explanation of events that occur with uniformity under the same conditions (e.g., laws of nature, law of gravitation).

Science is limited by the available technology. An example of this would be the relationship of the discovery of the cell to the invention of the microscope. As our technology improves, more hypotheses will become theories. Science is also limited by the data that we can collect. Data may be interpreted differently on different occasions. Science limitations cause explanations to be changeable as new technologies emerge.

The first step in scientific inquiry is posing a question. Next, a hypothesis is formed to provide a plausible explanation. An experiment is then proposed and performed to test this hypothesis. A comparison between the predicted and observed results is the next step. Conclusions are then formed and it is determined whether the hypothesis is correct or incorrect. If incorrect, the next step is to form a new hypothesis and repeat the process.

Better Response:

Science is derived from study, observations, and experimentation. The goal of science is to identify and establish principles and theories that may be applied to solve problems. Scientific theory and experimentation must be repeatable. It is also possible to disprove or change a theory. Science depends on communication, agreement, and disagreement among scientists.

A hypothesis is an educated guess followed by research. A theory is a hypothesis that has supporting experimentation. A theory is a principle or relationship that has been verified and accepted through experiments. A law is an explanation of events that occur with uniformity under the same conditions. Science is limited by the available technology. An example of this would be the relationship of the discovery of the cell to the invention of the microscope. The first step in scientific inquiry is posing a question. Next, a hypothesis is formed to provide a plausible explanation. An experiment is then proposed and performed to test this hypothesis. A comparison between the predicted and observed results is the next step. Conclusions are then formed and it is determined whether the hypothesis is correct or incorrect. If incorrect, the next step is to form a new hypothesis and repeat the process.

Basic Response:

Science is composed of hypotheses, theories, and laws. The first step in scientific inquiry is posing a question. Next, a hypothesis is formed to provide a plausible explanation. An experiment is then proposed and performed to test this hypothesis. A comparison between the predicted and observed results is the next step. Conclusions are then formed and it is determined whether the hypothesis is correct or incorrect. If incorrect, the next step is to form a new hypothesis and repeat the process. Science is always limited by the available technology.

Sample Test

Directions: Read each item and select the best response.

1. **Biological waste should be disposed of …**
   (Competency 001)(Easy)

   A. in the trash can.

   B. under a fume hood.

   C. in the broken glass box.

   D. in an autoclave biohazard bag.

2. **Chemicals should be stored (Competency 001)(Easy)**

   A. in a cool dark room.

   B. in a dark room.

   B. according to their reactivity with other substances.

   D. in a double locked room.

3. **The "Right to Know" law states …**
   (Competency 001)(Rigorous)

   A. the inventory of toxic chemicals checked against the "Substance List" must be available.

   B. that students are to be informed of alternatives to dissection.

   C. that science teachers are to be informed of student allergies.

   D. that students are to be informed of infectious microorganisms used in the lab.

4. **Which statement best defines negligence?**
   (Competency 001)(Average)

   A. failure to give oral instructions for those with reading disabilities

   B. failure to exercise ordinary care

   C. inability to supervise a large group of students

   D. reasonable anticipation that an event may occur

5. Which item should always be used when using chemicals with noxious vapors?
    (Competency 001)(Easy)

    A. eye protection

    B. face shield

    C. fume hood

    D. lab apron

6. A light microscope has an ocular of 10X and an objective of 40X. What is the total magnification?
    (Competency 001)(Rigorous)

    A. 400X

    B. 30X

    C. 50X

    D. 4000X

7. The reading of a meniscus in a graduated cylinder is done at the ...
    (Competency 001)(Easy)

    A. top of the meniscus.

    B. middle of the meniscus.

    C. bottom of the meniscus.

    D. closest whole number.

8. Spectrophotometry utilizes the principle of ...
    (Competency 001)(Average)

    A. light transmission.

    B. molecular weight.

    C. solubility of the substance.

    D. electrical charges.

9. A student designed a science project testing the effects of light and water on plant growth. You would recommend that she ...
    (Compensation 002)(Easy)

    A. manipulate the temperature as well.

    B. also alter the pH of the water as another variable.

    C. omit either water or light as a variable.

    D. also alter the light concentration as another variable.

10. Identify the control in the following experiment. A student grew four plants under the following conditions and measured photosynthetic rate by measuring mass. Two plants were grown in 50% light and two plants were grown in 100% light.
(Competency 002)(Easy)

A. plants grown with no added nutrients

B. plants grown in the dark

C. plants in 100% light

D. plants in 50% light

11. Potassium chloride is an example of a(n) ...
(Competency 004)(Average)

A. nonpolar covalent bond.

B. polar covalent bond.

C. ionic bond.

D. hydrogen bond.

12. Which of the following items are properties of water?
(Competency 004)(Rigorous)

I. High specific heat
II. Strong ionic bonds
III. Good solvent
IV. High freezing point

A. I, III, IV

B. II and III

C. I and II

D. II, III, IV

13. Which does not affect enzyme rate?
(Competency 004)(Average)

A. increase of temperature

B. amount of substrate

C. pH

D. size of the cell

14. What are the monomers in polysaccharides?
(Competency 004(Easy)

A. nucleotides

B. amino acids

C. polypeptides

D. simple sugars

15. In DNA, adenine bonds with
_____, while cytosine
bonds with _____.
(Competency 004)(Easy)

A. thymine/guanine

B. adenine/cytosine

C. cytosine/adenine

D. guanine/thymine

16. Which protein structure
consists of the coils and
folds of polypeptide chains?
(Competency 004)(Rigorous)

A. secondary structure

B. quaternary structure

C. tertiary structure

D. primary structure

17. Microorganisms use all but
the following to move ...
(Competency 005)(Rigorous)

A. pseudopods.

B. flagella.

C. cilia.

D. pilli.

18. Which is not a characteristic
of living things?
(Competency 005)(Average)

A. movement

B. cellular structure

C. metabolism

D. reproduction

19. Which kingdom is comprised
of organisms made of one
cell with no nuclear
membrane?
(Competency 005)(Easy)

A. Monera

B. Protista

C. Fungi

D. Algae

20. Rough endoplasmic
reticulum contains ...
(Competency 005)(Average)

A. vacuoles.

B. mitochondria.

C. microfilaments.

D. ribosomes .

21. The purpose of the Golgi apparatus is ...
(Competency 005)(Rigorous)

    A. to break down proteins.

    B. to sort, modify and package molecules.

    C. to break down fats.

    D. to make carbohydrates.

22. In the comparison of respiration to photosynthesis, which statement is true?
(Competency 005)(Rigorous)

    A. oxygen is a waste product in photosynthesis but not in respiration

    B. glucose is produced in respiration but not in photosynthesis

    C. carbon dioxide is formed in photosynthesis but not in respiration

    D. water is formed in respiration but not in photosynthesis

23. A virus that can remain dormant until a certain environmental condition causes its rapid increase is said to be ...
(Competency 005)(Average)

    A. lytic.

    B. benign.

    C. saprophytic.

    D. lysogenic.

24. Antibiotics are effective in fighting bacterial infections due to their ability to ...
(Competency 005)(Rigorous)

    A. interfere with DNA replication in the bacteria.

    B. prevent the formation of new cell walls in the bacteria.

    C. disrupt the ribosome of the bacteria.

    D. All of the above

25. Bacteria commonly reproduce by a process called binary fission. Which of the following best defines this process? (Competency 005)(Rigorous)

A. viral vectors carry DNA to new bacteria

B. DNA from one bacterium enters another

C. DNA doubles and the bacterial cell divides

D. DNA from dead cells is absorbed into bacteria

26. Using a gram staining technique, it is observed that E. coli stains pink. It is therefore ... (Competency 005)(Average)

A. gram positive.

B. dead.

C. gram negative.

D. gram neutral.

27. A genetic engineering advancement in the medical field is ... (Competency 005)(Rigorous)

A. gene therapy.

B. pesticides.

C. degradation of harmful chemicals.

D. antibiotics.

28. The shape of a cell depends on its ... (Competency 005)(Average)

A. function.

B. structure.

C. age.

D. size.

29. The most ATP is generated Through ... (Competency 005)(Rigorous)

A. fermentation.

B. glycolysis.

C. chemiosmosis.

D. the Krebs cycle.

30. The individual parts of cells are best studied using a(n) ... (Competency 005)(Average)

A. ultracentrifuge.

B. phase-contrast microscope.

C. CAT scan.

D. electron microscope.

31. Which of the following is not a type of fiber that makes up the cytoskeleton?
(Competency 005)(Average)

A. vacuoles

B. microfilaments

C. microtubules

D. intermediate filaments

32. Viruses are made of …
(Competency 005)(Rigorous)

A. a protein coat surrounding a nucleic acid.

B. DNA, RNA, and a cell wall.

C. a nucleic acid surrounding a protein coat.

D. protein surrounded by DNA.

33. The product of anaerobic respiration in animals is …
(Competency 006)(Rigorous)

A. carbon dioxide.

B. lactic acid.

C. pyruvate.

D. ethyl alcohol.

34. Carbon dioxide is fixed in the form of glucose in …
(Competency 006)(Rigorous)

A. the Krebs cycle.

B. the light reactions.

C. the dark reactions (Calvin cycle).

D. glycolysis.

35. During the Krebs cycle, 8 carrier molecules are formed. What are they?
(Competency 006)(Rigorous)

A. 3 NADH, 3 FADH, 2 ATP

B. 6 NADH and 2 ATP

C. 4 $FADH_2$ and 4 ATP

D. 6 NADH and 2 $FADH_2$

36. What is necessary for diffusion to occur?
(Competency 006)(Average)

A. carrier proteins

B. energy

C. a concentration gradient

D. a membrane

37. Which is an example of the use of energy to move a substance through a membrane from areas of low concentration to areas of high concentration?
(Competency 006)(Average)

A. osmosis

B. active transport

C. exocytosis

D. phagocytosis

38. A plant cell is placed in salt water. The resulting movement of water out of the cell is called ...
(Competency 006)(Average)

A. facilitated diffusion.

B. diffusion.

C. transpiration.

D. osmosis.

39. According to the fluid-mosaic model of the cell membrane, membranes are composed of ...
(Competency 006)(Rigorous)

A. phospholipid bilayers with proteins embedded in the layers.

B. one layer of phospholipids with cholesterol embedded in the layer.

C. two layers of protein with lipids embedded in the layers.

D. DNA and fluid proteins.

40. Oxygen is given off in the ...
(Competency 006)(Rigorous)

A. light reactions of photosynthesis.

B. dark reactions of photosynthesis.

C. Krebs cycle.

D. reduction of NAD+ to NADH.

41. In the electron transport chain, all the following are true except …
(Competency 006)(Rigorous)

   A. it occurs in the mitochondrion.

   B. it does not make ATP directly.

   C. the net gain of energy is 30 ATP.

   D. most molecules in the electron transport chain are proteins.

42. Facilitated diffusion …
(Competency 006)(Rigorous)

   A. requires energy.

   B. only happens in plant cells.

   C. requires a transport molecule to pass through the membrane.

   D. only allows molecules to leave a cell but no to enter it.

43. Which photosystem makes ATP?
(Competency 006)(Rigorous)

   A. photosystem I

   B. photosystem II

   C. photosystem III

   D. photosystem IV

44. Identify the correct sequence of organization of living things.
(Competency 007)(Easy)

   A. cell – organelle – organ – tissue – organ system – organism

   B. cell – tissue – organ – organelle – organ system – organism

   C. organelle – cell – tissue – organ – organ system – organism

   D. organ system – tissue – organelle – cell – organism – organ

45. The area of a DNA nucleotide that varies is the …
(Competency 008)(Rigorous)

   A. deoxyribose.

   B. phosphate group.

   C. nitrogenous base.

   D. sugar.

46. A DNA strand has the base sequence of TCAGTA. Its DNA complement would have the following sequence.
(Competency 008)(Average)

A. ATGACT

B. TCAGTA

C. AGUCAU

D. AGTCAT

47. Genes function in specifying the structure of which molecule?
(Competency 008)(Average)

A. carbohydrates

B. lipids

C. nucleic acids

D. proteins

48. What is the correct order of steps in protein synthesis?
(Competency 008)(Easy)

A. transcription, then replication

B. transcription, then translation

C. translation, then transcription

D. replication, then translation

49. This carries amino acids to the ribosome in protein synthesis.
(Competency 008)(Average)

A. messenger RNA

B. ribosomal RNA

C. transfer RNA

D. DNA

50. DNA synthesis results in a strand that is synthesized continuously. This is the …
(Competency 008)(Rigorous)

A. lagging strand.

B. leading strand.

C. template strand.

D. complementary strand.

51. Homozygous individuals …
(Competency 009)(Easy)

A. have two different alleles.

B. are of the same species.

C. have the same features.

D. have a pair of identical alleles.

52. Replication of chromosomes occurs during which phase of the cell cycle? (Competency 009)(Average)

A. prophase

B. interphase

C. metaphase

D. anaphase

53. Which statement regarding mitosis is correct? (Competency 009)(Rigorous)

A. diploid cells produce haploid cells for sexual reproduction

B. sperm and egg cells are produced

C. diploid cells produce diploid cells for growth and repair

D. it allows for greater genetic diversity

54. Identify this stage of mitosis. (Competency 009)(Average)

A. anaphase

B. metaphase

C. telophase

D. prophase

55. Identify this stage of mitosis. (Competency 009)(Average)

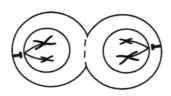

A. prophase

B. telophase

C. anaphase

D. metaphase

56. **Identify this stage of mitosis.**
(Competency 009)(Average)

A. anaphase

B. metaphase

C. prophase

D. telophase

57. **The term "phenotype" refers to which of the following? (Competency 009)(Rigorous)**

A. a condition which is heterozygous

B. the genetic makeup of an individual

C. a condition which is homozygous

D. how the genotype is expressed

58. **The Law of Segregation defined by Mendel states that ... (Competency 009)(Rigorous)**

A. when sex cells form, the two alleles that determine a trait will end up on different gametes.

B. only one of two alleles is expressed in a heterozygous organism.

C. the allele expressed is the dominant allele.

D. alleles of one trait do not affect the inheritance of alleles on another chromosome.

59. **When a white flower is crossed with a red flower, incomplete dominance can be seen by the production of which of the following? (Competency 009)(Average)**

A. pink flowers

B. red flowers

C. white flowers

D. red and white flowers

60. Amniocentesis is ...
(Competency 009)(Easy)

A. a non-invasive technique for detecting genetic disorders.

B. a bacterial infection.

C. extraction of amniotic fluid.

D. removal of fetal tissue.

61. A child with type O blood has a father with type A blood and a mother with type B blood. The genotypes of the parents respectively would be which of the following?
(Competency 009)(Average)

A. AA and BO

B. AO and BO

C. AA and BB

D. AO and OO

62. Any change that affects the sequence of bases in a gene is called a ...
(Competency 009)(Average)

A. deletion.

B. polyploid.

C. mutation.

D. duplication.

63. Which process(es) result(s) in a haploid chromosome number?
(Competency 009)(Easy)

A. both meiosis and mitosis

B. mitosis

C. meiosis

D. replication and division

64. Segments of DNA can be transferred from the DNA of one organism to another through the use of which of the following?
(Competency 009)(Rigorous)

A. bacterial plasmids

B. viruses

C. chromosomes from frogs

D. plant DNA

65. Which of the following factors will affect the Hardy-Weinberg law of equilibrium, leading to evolutionary change?
(Competency 010)(Average)

A. no mutations

B. non-random mating

C. no immigration or emigration

D. large population

66. Crossing over, which increases genetic diversity occurs during which stage(s)?
(Competency 010)(Average)

   A. telophase II in meiosis

   B. metaphase in mitosis

   C. interphase in both mitosis and meiosis

   D. prophase I in meiosis

67. The biological species concept applies to ...
(Competency 010)(Rigorous)

   A. asexual organisms.

   B. extinct organisms.

   C. sexual organisms.

   D. fossil organisms.

68. Reproductive isolation results in
(Competency 010)(Average)

   A. extinction.

   B. migration.

   C. follilization.

   D. speciation.

69. The Endosymbiotic theory states that ...
(Competency 011)(Rigorous)

   A. eukaryotes arose from prokaryotes.

   B. animals evolved in close relationships with one another.

   C. the prokaryotes arose from eukaryotes.

   D. life arose from inorganic compounds.

70. Evolution occurs in ...
(Competency 011)(Average)

   A. individuals.

   B. populations.

   C. organ systems.

   D. cells.

71. The wing of a bird, human arm, and whale flipper have the same bone structure. These are called
(Competency 012)(Average)

   A. polymorphic structures.

   B. homologous structures.

   C. vestigial structures.

   D. analogous structures.

72. **Which biome is the most prevalent on Earth?**
(Competency 012)(Easy)

A. marine

B. desert

C. savanna

D. tundra

73. **The two major ways to determine taxonomic classification are ...**
(Competency 12)(Rigorous)

A. evolution and phylogeny.

B. reproductive success and evolution.

C. phylogeny and morphology.

D. size and color.

74. **Man's scientific name is _Homo sapiens_. Choose the proper classification beginning with kingdom and ending with order.**
(Competency 12)(Rigorous)

A. Animalia, Vertebrata, Mammalia, Primate, Hominidae

B. Animalia, Vertebrata, Chordata, Mammalia, Primate

C. Animalia, Chordata, Vertebrata, Mammalia, Primate

D. Chordata, Vertebrata, Primate, Homo, sapiens

75. **Members of the same Species ...**
(Competency 12)(Easy)

A. look identical.

B. never change.

C. reproduce successfully within their group.

D. live in the same geographic location.

76. Water movement to the top of a twenty foot tree is most likely due to which principle? (Competency 013)(Average)

A. osmostic pressure

B. xylem pressure

C. capillarity

D. transpiration

77. What is not true of enzymes? (Competency 013)(Rigorous)

A. they are the most diverse of all proteins

B. they act on a substrate

C. they work at a wide range of pHs

D. they are temperature-dependent

78. What controls gas exchange on the bottom of a plant leaf? (Competency 013)(Average)

A. stomata

B. epidermis

C. collenchyma and schlerenchyma

D. palisade mesophyll

79. The function of the cardiovascular system is to: (Competency 013)(Average)

A. move oxygenated blood around the body via a pump and tubes.

B. to oxygenate the blood through gas exchange.

C. to act as an exocrine system.

D. to flush toxins out of the body.

80. Parts of the nervous system include all but the following: (Competency 013)(Easy)

A. brain

B. spinal cord

C. axons

D. venules

81. Which phylum accounts for 85% of all animal species? (Competency 013)(Average)

A. Nematoda

B. Chordata

C. Arthropoda

D. Cnidaria

82. **Which is the correct statement regarding the human nervous system and the human endocrine system?**
(Competency 013)(Rigorous)

A. the nervous system maintains homeostasis whereas the endocrine system does not

B. endocrine glands produce neurotransmitters whereas nerves produce hormones

C. nerve signals travel on neurons whereas hormones travel through the blood

D. the nervous system involves chemical transmission whereas the endocrine system does not

83. **A muscular adaptation to move food through the digestive system is called ...**
(Competency 013)(Easy)

A. peristalsis.

B. passive transport.

C. voluntary action.

D. bulk transport.

84. **The role of neurotransmitters in nerve action is**
(Competency 013)(Rigorous)

A. to turn off the sodium pump.

B. to turn off the calcium pump.

C. to send impulses to neurons.

D. to send impulses to the body.

85. **Fertilization in humans usually occurs in the ...**
(Competency 13)(Average)

A. uterus.

B. ovary.

C. fallopian tubes.

D. vagina.

86. **All of the following are found in the dermis layer of skin except ...**
(Competency 013)(Average)

A. sweat glands.

B. keratin.

C. hair follicles.

D. blood vessels.

87. Movement is possible by the action of muscles pulling on..
(Competency 013)(Easy)

A. skin.

B. bones.

C. joints.

D. ligaments.

88. All of the following are functions of the skin except ..
(Competency 013)(Average)

A. storage.

B. protection.

C. sensation.

D. regulation of temperature.

89. Hormones are essential to the regulation of reproduction. What organ is responsible for the release of hormones for sexual maturity?
(Competency 013)(Average)

A. pituitary gland

B. hypothalamus

C. pancreas

D. thyroid gland

90. A school age boy had the chicken pox as a baby. He will most likely not get this disease again because of...
(Competency 013)(Average)

A. passive immunity.

B. vaccination.

C. antibiotics.

D. active immunity.

91. The body's endocrine mechanisms are controlled by ...
(Competency 013) (Average)

A. feedback loops.

B. control molecules.

C. neurochemicals.

D. neurotransmitters.

92. The most common neurotransmitter is...
(Competency 013)(Average)

A. epinephrine.

B. serotonin.

C. Acetyl choline.

D. norepinephrine.

93. Homeostatic mechanisms in the body include all but the following …
(Competency 014)(Rigorous)

A. thermoregulation

B. excretion

C. respiration

D. osmoregulation

94. After sea turtles hatched on the beach, they start the journey to the ocean. This is due to …
(Competency 015)(Average)

A. innate behavior.

B. territoriality.

C. the tide.

D. learned behavior.

95. Which term is not associated with the water cycle?
(Competency 016)(Average)

A. precipitation

B. transpiration

C. fixation

D. evaporation

96. All of the following are density independent factors that affect a population except …
(Competency 017)(Average)

A. temperature.

B. rainfall.

C. predation.

D. soil nutrients.

97. Which trophic level has the highest ecological efficiency?
(Competency 017)(Average)

A. decomposers

B. producers

C. tertiary consumers

D. secondary consumers

98. In the growth of a population, the increase is exponential until carrying capacity is reached. This is represented by a(n) …
(Competition 018)(Rigorous)

A. S curve.

B. J curve.

C. M curve.

D. L curve.

99. **Primary succession occurs after
(Competency 018)(Rigorous)**

    A. nutrient enrichment.

    B. a forest fire.

    C. bare rock is exposed after a water table recedes.

    D. a housing development is built.

100. **A clownfish is protected by the sea anemone's tentacles. In turn, the anemone receives uneaten food from the clownfish. This is an example of
(Competency 018)(Rigorous)**

    A. mutualism.

    B. parasitism.

    C. commensalism.

    D. competition.

Answer Key

1. D	45. C	89. B
2. C	46. D	90. D
3. A	47. D	91. A
4. B	48. B	92. C
5. C	49. C	93. C
6. A	50. B	94. A
7. C	51. D	95. C
8. A	52. B	96. C
9. C	53. C	97. B
10. C	54. B	98. A
11. C	55. B	99. C
12. A	56. A	100. A
13. D	57. D	
14. D	58. A	
15. A	59. A	
16. A	60. C	
17. D	61. B	
18. A	62. C	
19. A	63. C	
20. D	64. A	
21. B	65. B	
22. A	66. D	
23. D	67. C	
24. D	68. D	
25. C	69. A	
26. C	70. B	
27. A	71. B	
28. A	72. A	
29. C	73. C	
30. D	74. C	
31. A	75. C	
32. A	76. D	
33. B	77. C	
34. C	78. A	
35. D	79. A	
36. C	80. D	
37. B	81. C	
38. D	82. C	
39. A	83. A	
40. A	84. A	
41. C	85. C	
42. C	86. B	
43. A	87. B	
44. C	88. A	

Rigor Table

Easy Rigor 20%	Average Rigor 40%	Rigorous 40%
1, 2, 5, 7, 9, 10, 14, 15, 19, 44, 48, 51, 60, 63, 72, 75, 80, 83, 87	4, 8, 11, 13, 18, 20, 23, 26, 28, 30, 31, 36, 37, 38, 46, 47, 49, 52, 54, 55, 56, 59, 61, 62, 65, 66, 68, 70, 71, 76, 78, 79, 81, 85, 86, 88, 89, 90, 91, 92, 94, 95, 96, 97	3, 6, 12, 16, 17, 21, 22, 24, 25, 27, 29, 32, 33, 34, 35, 39, 40, 41, 42, 43, 45, 50, 53, 57, 58, 64, 67, 69, 73, 74, 77, 82, 84, 93, 98, 99, 100

Rationales with Sample Questions

1. **Biological waste should be disposed of ... (Competency 001)(Easy)**

   A. in the trash can.
   B. under a fume hood.
   C. in the broken glass box.
   D. in an autoclave biohazard bag.

Answer: D. in an autoclave biohazard bag
Biological material should never be stored near food or water used for human consumption. All biological material should be appropriately labeled. All blood and body fluids should be put in a well-contained container with a secure lid to prevent leaking. All biological waste should be disposed of in biological hazardous waste bags.

2. **Chemicals should be stored ... (Competency 001)(Easy)**

   A. in a cool dark room.
   B. in a dark room.
   C. according to their reactivity with other substances.
   D. in a double locked room.

Answer: C. according to their reactivity with other substances
All chemicals should be stored with other chemicals of similar reactivity. Failure to do so could result in an undesirable chemical reaction.

3. **The "Right to Know" law states ... (Competency 001)(Rigorous)**

   A. the inventory of toxic chemicals checked against the "Substance List" be available.
   B. that students are to be informed of alternatives to dissection.
   C. that science teachers are to be informed of student allergies.
   D. that students are to be informed of infectious microorganisms used in lab.

Answer: A. the inventory of toxic chemicals checked against the "Substance List" be available
The right to know law pertains to chemical substances in the lab. Employees should check the material safety data sheets and the substance list for potential hazards in the lab.

4. Which statement best defines negligence? (Competency 001)(Average)

A. failure to give oral instructions for those with reading disabilities
B. failure to exercise ordinary care
C. inability to supervise a large group of students
D. reasonable anticipation that an event may occur

Answer: B. failure to exercise ordinary care
Negligence is the failure to exercise ordinary or reasonable care.

5. Which item should always be used when using chemicals with noxious vapors? (Competency 001)(Easy)

A. eye protection
B. face shield
C. fume hood
D. lab apron

Answer: C. fume hood
Fume hoods are designed to protect the experimenter from chemical fumes. The three other choices do not prevent chemical fumes from entering the respiratory system.

6. A light microscope has an ocular of 10X and an objective of 40X. What is the total magnification?(Competency 001)(Rigorous)

A. 400X
B. 30X
C. 50X
D. 4000X

Answer: A. 400x
To determine the total magnification of a microscope, multiply the ocular lens by the objective lens. Here, the ocular lens is 10X and the objective lens is 40X.

(10X) X (40X) = 400X total magnification

7. **The reading of a meniscus in a graduated cylinder is done at the ...**
   (Competency 001)(Easy)

   A. top of the meniscus.
   B. middle of the meniscus.
   C. bottom of the meniscus.
   D. closest whole number.

Answer: C. bottom of the meniscus
The graduated cylinder is a common instrument used for measuring volume. It is important for the accuracy of the measurement to read the volume level of the liquid at the bottom of the meniscus. The meniscus is the curved surface of the liquid.

8. **Spectrophotometry utilizes the principle of ...**
   (Competency 001)(Average)

   A. light transmission.
   B. molecular weight.
   C. solubility of the substance.
   D. electrical charges.

Answer: A. light transmission
Spectrophotometry uses percent of light at different wavelengths absorbed and transmitted by a pigment solution.

9. **A student designed a science experiment testing the effects of light and water on plant growth. You would recommend that she ...**
   (Competency 002)(Easy)

   A. manipulate the temperature as well.
   B. also alter the pH of the water as another variable.
   C. omit either water or light as a variable.
   D. also alter the light concentration as another variable.

Answer: C. omit either water or light as a variable
In science, experiments should be designed so that only one variable is manipulated at a time.

10. **Identify the control in the following experiment. A student grew four plants under the following conditions and was measuring photosynthetic rate by measuring mass. 2 plants in 50% light and 2 plants in 100% light. (Competency 002)(Easy)**

    A. plants grown with no added nutrients
    B. plants grown in the dark
    C plants in 100% light
    D. plants in 50% light

Answer: C. plants in 100% light
The 100% light plants are those that the student will be comparing the 50% plants to. This will be the control.

11. **Potassium chloride is an example of a(n) ... (Competency 004)(Average)**

    A. nonpolar covalent bond.
    B. polar covalent bond.
    C. ionic bond.
    D. hydrogen bond.

Answer: C. ionic bond
Ionic bonds are formed when one electron is stripped away from its atom to join another atom. Ionic compounds are called salts and potassium chloride is a salt; therefore, potassium chloride is an example of an ionic bond.

12. **Which of the following are properties of water? (Competency 004)(Rigorous)**

    I. High specific heat
    II. Strong ionic bonds
    III.Good solvent
    IV.High freezing point

    A. I, III, IV
    B. II and III
    C. I and II
    D. II, III, IV

Answer: A. I, III, IV
All are properties of water except strong ionic bonds. Water is held together by polar covalent bonds between hydrogen and oxygen.

13. Which does not affect enzyme rate? (Competency 004)(Average)

A. increase of temperature
B. amount of substrate
C. pH
D. size of the cell

Answer: D. size of the cell
Temperature and pH can affect the rate of reaction of an enzyme. The amount of substrate affects the enzyme as well. The enzyme acts on the substrate. The more substrate, the faster the enzyme rate. Therefore, the only choice left is D, the size of the cell, which has no effect on enzyme rate.

14. What are the monomers in polysaccharides? (Competency 004)(Easy)

A. Nucleotides
B. Amino acids
C. Polypeptides
D. Simple sugars

Answer: D. simple sugars
The monomers of polysaccharides are simple sugars.

15. In DNA, adenine bonds with _____, while cytosine bonds with _____. (Competency 004)(Easy)

A. thymine/guanine
B. adenine/cytosine
C. cytosine/adenine
D. guanine/thymine

Answer: A. thymine/guanine
In DNA, adenine pairs with thymine and cytosine pairs with guanine because of their nitrogenous base structures.

16. **Which protein structure consists of the coils and folds of polypeptide chains?(Competency 004)(Rigorous)**

   A. secondary structure
   B. quaternary structure
   C. tertiary structure
   D. primary structure

Answer: A. secondary structure
Primary structure is the protein's unique sequence of amino acids. Secondary structure is the coils and folds of polypeptide chains. The coils and folds are the result of hydrogen bonds along the polypeptide backbone. Tertiary structure is formed by bonding between the side chains of the amino acids. Quaternary structure is the overall structure of the protein from the aggregation of two or more polypeptide chains.

17. **Microorganisms use all but the following to move …
   (Competency 005)(Rigorous)**

   A. pseudopods
   B. flagella
   C. cilia
   D. pili

Answer: D. pili
Pseudopods, flagella and cilia are used by microorganisms for movement. Pili are used for attachment.

18. **Which is not a characteristic of living things?
   (Competency 005)(Average)**

   A. movement
   B. cellular structure
   C. metabolism
   D. reproduction

Answer: A. movement
Movement is not a characteristic of all life.

19. **Which kingdom is comprised of organisms made of one cell with no nuclear membrane? (Competency 005)(Easy)**

    A. Monera
    B. Protista
    C. Fungi
    D. Algae

Answer: A. monera
Monera is the only kingdom that is made up of unicellular organisms with no nucleus. Algae is a protist because it is made up of one type of tissue and it has a nucleus.

20. **Rough endoplasmic reticulum contains ... (Competency 005)(Average)**

    A. vacuoles
    B. mitochondria
    C. microfilaments
    D. ribosomes

Answer: D. ribosomes
Rough endoplasmic reticulum is defined as such because of the occurrence of ribosomes on its surface

21. **The purpose of the Golgi Apparatus is ... (Competency 005)(Rigorous)**

    A. To break down proteins
    B. To sort, modify and package molecules
    C. To break down fats
    D. To make carbohydrates.

Answer: B. to sort, modify and package molecules
The Golgi Apparatus takes molecules from the endoplasmic reticulum and sorts, modifies and packages the molecules for later use by the cell.

22. **In the comparison of respiration to photosynthesis, which statement is true? (Competency 005)(Rigorous)**

    A. oxygen is a waste product in photosynthesis but not in respiration
    B. glucose is produced in respiration but not in photosynthesis
    C. carbon dioxide is formed in photosynthesis but not in respiration
    D. water is formed in respiration but not in photosynthesis

Answer: A.   oxygen is a waste product in photosynthesis but not in respiration

In photosynthesis, water is split and the oxygen is given off as a waste product. In respiration, water and carbon dioxide are the waste products.

23. **A virus that can remain dormant until a certain environmental condition causes its rapid increase is said to be … (Competency 005)(Average)**

    A. lytic.
    B. benign.
    C. saprophytic.
    D. lysogenic.

Answer: D. lysogenic

Lysogenic viruses remain dormant until something initiates it to break out of the host cell.

24. **Antibiotics are effective in fighting bacterial infections due to their ability to … (Competency 005)(Rigorous)**

    A. interfere with DNA replication in the bacteria.
    B. prevent the formation of new cell wall in the bacteria.
    C. disrupt the ribosome of the bacteria.
    D. All of the above.

Answer: D. All of the above

Various antibiotics can destroy the bacterial cell wall, interfere with bacterial DNA replication, and disrupt the bacterial ribosome without affecting the host cells.

25. **Bacteria commonly reproduce by a process called binary fission. Which of the following best defines this process? (Competency 005)(Rigorous)**

    A. viral vectors carry DNA to new bacteria
    B. DNA from one bacterium enters another
    C. DNA doubles and the bacterial cell divides
    D. DNA from dead cells is absorbed into bacteria

Answer: C. DNA doubles and the bacterial cell divides
Binary fission is the asexual process in which the bacteria divide in half after the DNA doubles. This results in an exact genetic clone of the parent cell.

26. **Using a gram staining technique, it is observed that *E. coli* stains pink. It is therefore ... (Competency 005)(Average)**

    A. gram positive.
    B. dead.
    C. gram negative.
    D. gram neutral.

Answer: C. gram negative
A Gram positive bacterium absorbs the stain and appears purple under a microscope because of its cell wall made of peptidoglycan. A Gram negative bacterium does not absorb the stain as well because of its more complex cell wall. These bacteria appear pink under a microscope.

27. **A genetic engineering advancement in the medical field is ... (Competency 005)(Rigorous)**

    A. gene therapy.
    B. pesticides.
    C. degradation of harmful chemicals.
    D. antibiotics.

Answer: A. gene therapy
Gene therapy is the introduction of a normal allele to the somatic cells to replace a defective allele. The medical field has had limited success in treating patients with a single enzyme deficiency disease. Gene therapy has allowed doctors and scientists to introduce a normal allele that provides the missing enzyme.

28. The shape of a cell depends on its … (Competency 005)(Average)

    A. function.
    B. structure.
    C. age.
    D. size.

Answer: A. function
In most living organisms, cellular structure is based on function.

29. The most ATP is generated through … (Competency 005)(Rigorous)

    A. fermentation.
    B. glycolysis.
    C. chemiosmosis.
    D. the Krebs cycle.

Answer: C. chemiosmosis
The electron transport chain uses electrons to pump hydrogen ions across the mitochondrial membrane. This ion gradient is used to form ATP in a process called chemiosmosis. ATP is generated by the removal of hydrogen ions from NADH and $FADH_2$. This yields about 34 ATP molecules.

30. The individual parts of cells are best studied using a(n) … (Competency 005)(Average)

    A. ultracentrifuge.
    B. phase-contrast microscope.
    C. CAT scan.
    D. electron microscope.

Answer: D. electron microscope
The transmission electron microscope uses a beam of electrons to pass through the specimen. The resolution is about 1000 times greater than that of a light microscope. This allows the scientist to view extremely small objects, such as the individual parts of a cell.

31. **Which of the following is not a type of fiber that makes up the cytoskeleton? (Competency 005)(Average)**

    A. vacuoles
    B. microfilaments
    C. microtubules
    D. intermediate filaments

Answer: A. vacuoles
Vacuoles are mostly found in plants and hold stored food and pigments. The other three choices are fibers that make up the cytoskeleton found in both plant and animal cells.

32. **Viruses are made of ... (Competency 005)(Rigorous)**

    A. a protein coat surrounding a nucleic acid.
    B. DNA, RNA, and a cell wall.
    C. a nucleic acid surrounding a protein coat.
    D. protein surrounded by DNA.

Answer: A. a protein coat surrounding a nucleic acid
Viruses are composed of a protein coat and a nucleic acid; either RNA or DNA.

33. **The product of anaerobic respiration in animals is ... (Competency 006)(Rigorous)**

    A. carbon dioxide.
    B. lactic acid.
    C. pyruvate.
    D. ethyl alcohol.

Answer: B. lactic acid
In anaerobic lactic acid fermentation, pyruvate is reduced by NADH to form lactic acid. This is the anaerobic process in animals. Alcoholic fermentation is the anaerobic process in yeast and some bacteria resulting in ethyl alcohol. Carbon dioxide and pyruvate are the products of aerobic respiration.

34. Carbon dioxide is fixed in the form of glucose in … (Competency 006)(Rigorous)

    A. the Krebs cycle.
    B. the light reactions.
    C. the dark reactions (Calvin cycle).
    D. glycolysis.

Answer: C. the dark reactions (Calvin cycle)
The ATP produced during the light reaction is needed to convert carbon dioxide to glucose in the Calvin cycle.

35. During the Krebs cycle, 8 carrier molecules are formed. What are they? (Competency 006)(Average)

    A. 3 NADH, 3 FADH, 2 ATP
    B. 6 NADH and 2 ATP
    C. 4 $FADH_2$ and 4 ATP
    D. 6 NADH and 2 $FADH_2$

Answer: D. 6 NADH and 2 $FADH_2$
For each molecule of CoA that enters the Kreb's cycle, you get 3 NADH and 1 $FADH_2$. There are 2 molecules of CoA formed from each glucose so the total yield is 6 NADH and 2 $FADH_2$ during the Krebs cycle.

36. What is necessary for diffusion to occur? (Competency 006)(Average)

    A. carrier proteins
    B. energy
    C. a concentration gradient
    D. a membrane

Answer: C. a concentration gradient
Diffusion is the ability of molecules to move from areas of high concentration to areas of low concentration (a concentration gradient).

37. **Which is an example of the use of energy to move a substance through a membrane from areas of low concentration to areas of high concentration? (Competency 006)(Average)**

    A. osmosis
    B. active transport
    C. exocytosis
    D. phagocytosis

Answer: B. active transport
Active transport can move substances with or against the concentration gradient. This energy-requiring process allows for molecules to be moved from areas of low concentration to areas of high concentration.

38. **A plant cell is placed in salt water. The resulting movement of water out of the cell is called ... (Competency 006)(Average)**

    A. facilitated diffusion.
    B. diffusion.
    C. transpiration.
    D. osmosis.

Answer: D. osmosis
Osmosis is simply the diffusion of water across a semi-permeable membrane. Water will diffuse out of the cell if there is less water on the outside of the cell.

39. **According to the fluid-mosaic model of the cell membrane, membranes are composed of ... (Competency 006)(Rigorous)**

    A. phospholipid bilayers with proteins embedded in the layers.
    B. one layer of phospholipids with cholesterol embedded in the layer.
    C. two layers of protein with lipids embedded the layers.
    D. DNA and fluid proteins.

Answer: A. phospholipid bilayers with proteins embedded in the layers
Cell membranes are composed of two phospholipids with their hydrophobic tails sandwiched between their hydrophilic heads, creating a lipid bilayer. The membrane contains proteins embedded in the layer (integral proteins) and proteins on the surface (peripheral proteins).

40. Oxygen is given off in the... (Competency 006)(Rigorous)

 A. light reactions of photosynthesis.
 B. dark reactions of photosynthesis.
 C. Krebs cycle.
 D. reduction of NAD+ to NADH.

Answer: A. light reactions of photosynthesis
The conversion of solar energy to chemical energy occurs in the light reactions. Electrons are transferred by the absorption of light by chlorophyll and cause water to split, releasing oxygen as a waste product.

41. In the electron transport chain, all the following are true except... (Competency 006)(Rigorous)

 A. it occurs in the mitochondrion.
 B. it does not make ATP directly.
 C. the net gain of energy is 30 ATP.
 D. most molecules in the electron transport chain are proteins.

Answer: C. the net gain of energy is 30 ATP
The end result of the electron transport chain is 34 molecules of ATP.

42. Facilitated diffusion: (Competency 006)(Rigorous)

 A. Requires energy
 B. Only happens in plant cells
 C. Requires a transport molecule to pass through the membrane.
 D. Only allows molecules to leave a cell but no to enter it.

Answer: C. requires a transport molecule to pass through the membrane
Facilitated diffusion requires no energy but need a transport molecule to pass another molecule through the membrane.

43. **Which photosystem makes ATP?**
    (Competency 006)(Rigorous)

    A. photosystem I
    B. photosystem II
    C. photosystem III
    D. photosystem IV

Answer: A. photosystem I
Photosystem I is composed of a pair of chlorophyll *a* molecules It makes ATP whose energy is needed to build glucose.

44. **Identify the correct sequence of organization of living things.**
    (Competency 007)(Easy)

    A. cell – organelle – organ system – tissue – organ – organism
    B. cell – tissue – organ – organ system – organelle – organism
    C. organelle – cell – tissue – organ – organ system – organism
    D. tissue – organelle – organ – cell – organism – organ system

Answer: C. organelle – cell – tissue – organ – organ system – organism
An organism, such as a human, is comprised of several organ systems such as the circulatory and nervous systems. These organ systems consist of many organs including the heart and the brain. These organs are made of tissue such as cardiac muscle. Tissues are made up of cells, which contain organelles like the mitochondria and the Golgi apparatus.

45. **The area of a DNA nucleotide that varies is the...**
    (Competency 008)(Rigorous)

    A. deoxyribose.
    B. phosphate group.
    C. nitrogenous base.
    D. sugar.

Answer: C. nitrogenous base
DNA is made of a 5-carbon sugar (deoxyribose), a phosphate group, and a nitrogenous base. There are four nitrogenous bases in DNA that allow for the four different nucleotides.

46. A DNA strand has the base sequence of TCAGTA. Its DNA complement would have the following sequence. (Competency 008)(Average)

   A. ATGACT
   B. TCAGTA
   C. AGUCAU
   D. AGTCAT

Answer: D. AGTCAT
The complement strand to a single strand DNA molecule has a complementary sequence to the template strand. T pairs with A and C pairs with G. Therefore, the complement to TCAGTA is AGTCAT.

47. Genes function in specifying the structure of which molecule? (Competency 008)(Average)

   A. carbohydrates
   B. lipids
   C. nucleic acids
   D. proteins

Answer: D. proteins
Genes contain the sequence of nucleotides that code for amino acids. Amino acids are the building blocks of protein.

48. What is the correct order of steps in protein synthesis? (Competency 008)(Easy)

   A. transcription, then replication
   B. transcription, then translation
   C. translation, then transcription
   D. replication, then translation

Answer: B. transcription, then translation
A DNA strand first undergoes transcription to get a complementary mRNA strand. Translation of the mRNA strand then occurs to result in the tRNA adding the appropriate amino acid for an end product, a protein.

49. **This carries amino acids to the ribosome in protein synthesis. (Competency 008)(Average)**

   A. messenger RNA
   B. ribosomal RNA
   C. transfer RNA
   D. DNA

Answer: C. transfer RNA
The tRNA molecule is specific for a particular amino acid. The tRNA has an anticodon sequence that is complementary to the codon. This specifies where the tRNA places the amino acid in protein synthesis.

50. **DNA synthesis results in a strand that is synthesized continuously. This is the... (Competency 008)(Rigorous)**

   A. lagging strand.
   B. leading strand.
   C. template strand.
   D. complementary strand.

Answer: B. leading strand
As DNA synthesis proceeds along the replication fork, one strand is replicated continuously (the leading strand) and the other strand is replicated discontinuously (the lagging strand).

51. **Homozygous individuals... (Competency 009)(Easy)**

   A. have two different alleles.
   B. are of the same species.
   C. have the same features.
   D. have a pair of identical alleles.

Answer: D. have a pair of identical alleles
Homozygous individuals have a pair of identical alleles and heterozygous individuals have two different alleles.

52. **Replication of chromosomes occurs during which phase of the cell cycle?(Competency 009)(Average)**

    A. prophase
    B. interphase
    C. metaphase
    D. anaphase

Answer: B. interphase
Interphase is the stage where the cell grows and copies the chromosomes in preparation for the mitotic phase.

53. **Which statement regarding mitosis is correct?
    (Competency 009)(Rigorous)**

    A. diploid cells produce haploid cells for sexual reproduction
    B. sperm and egg cells are produced
    C. diploid cells produce diploid cells for growth and repair
    D. it allows for greater genetic diversity

Answer: C. diploid cells produce diploid cells for growth and repair
The purpose of mitotic cell division is to provide growth and repair in body (somatic) cells. The cells begin as diploid and produce diploid cells.

54. **Identify this stage of mitosis. (Competency 009)(Average)**

    A. anaphase
    B. metaphase
    C. telophase
    D. prophase

Answer: B. metaphase
During metaphase, the centromeres are at opposite ends of the cell. Here the chromosomes are aligned with one another.

55. Identify this stage of mitosis. (Competency 009)(Average)

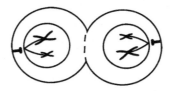

    A. prophase
    B. telophase
    C. anaphase
    D. metaphase

Answer: B. telophase
Telophase is the last stage of mitosis. Here, two nuclei become visible and the nuclear membrane reassembles.

56. Identify this stage of mitosis. (Competency 009)(Average)

    A. anaphase
    B. metaphase
    C. prophase
    D. telophase

Answer: A. anaphase
During anaphase, the centromeres split in half and homologous chromosomes separate.

57. The term "phenotype" refers to which of the following? (Competency 009)(Rigorous)

    A. a condition which is heterozygous
    B. the genetic makeup of an individual
    C. a condition which is homozygous
    D. how the genotype is expressed

Answer: D. how the genotype is expressed
Phenotype is the physical appearance of an organism due to its genetic makeup (genotype).

58. **The Law of Segregation defined by Mendel states that ...**
    (Competency 009)(Rigorous)

    A. when sex cells form, the two alleles that determine a trait will end up on different gametes.
    B. only one of two alleles is expressed in a heterozygous organism.
    C. the allele expressed is the dominant allele.
    D. alleles of one trait do not affect the inheritance of alleles on another Chromosome.

Answer: A. when sex cells form, the two alleles that determine a trait will end up on different gametes
The law of segregation states that the two alleles for each trait segregate into different gametes.

59. **When a white flower is crossed with a red flower, incomplete dominance can be seen by the production of which of the following? (Competency 009)(Average)**

    A. pink flowers
    B. red flowers
    C. white flowers
    D. red and white flowers

Answer: A. pink flowers
Incomplete dominance is when the F_1 generation results in an appearance somewhere between the parents. Red flowers crossed with white flowers results in an F_1 generation with pink flowers.

60. **Amniocentesis is ... (Competency 009)(Easy)**

    A. a non-invasive technique for detecting genetic disorders.
    B. a bacterial infection.
    C. extraction of amniotic fluid.
    D. removal of fetal tissue.

Answer: C. extraction of amniotic fluid
Amniocentesis is a procedure in which a needle is inserted into the uterus to extract some of the amniotic fluid surrounding the fetus. Some genetic disorders can be detected by chemicals in the fluid.

61. **A child with type O blood has a father with type A blood and a mother with type B blood. The genotypes of the parents respectively would be which of the following? (Competency 009)(Average)**

   A. AA and BO
   B. AO and BO
   C. AA and BB
   D. AO and OO

Answer: B. AO and BO
Type O blood has 2 recessive O genes. A child receives one allele from each parent; therefore, each parent in this example must have an O allele. The father has type A blood with a genotype of AO and the mother has type B blood with a genotype of BO.

62. **Any change that affects the sequence of bases in a gene is called a(n) ... (Competency 009)(Average)**

   A. deletion.
   B. polyploidy.
   C. mutation.
   D. duplication.

Answer: C. mutation
A mutation is an inheritable change in DNA. It may be an error in replication or a spontaneous rearrangement of one or more segments of DNA. Deletion and duplication are types of mutations. Polyploidy is when and organism has more than two complete chromosome sets.

63. **Which process(es) result(s) in a haploid chromosome number? (Competency 009)(Easy)**

   A. both meiosis and mitosis
   B. mitosis
   C. meiosis
   D. replication and division

Answer: C. meiosis
In meiosis, there are two consecutive cell divisions resulting in the reduction of the chromosome number by half (diploid to haploid).

64. **Segments of DNA can be transferred from the DNA of one organism to another through the use of which of the following? (Competency 009)(Rigorous)**

   A. bacterial plasmids
   B. viruses
   C. chromosomes from frogs
   D. plant DNA

Answer: A. bacterial plasmids
Plasmids can transfer themselves (and therefore their genetic information) by a process called conjugation. This requires cell-to-cell contact.

65. **Which of the following factors will affect the Hardy-Weinberg law of equilibrium, leading to evolutionary change? (Competency 010)(Average)**

   A. no mutations
   B. non-random mating
   C. no immigration or emigration
   D. large population

Answer: B. non-random mating
There are five requirements to keep the Hardy-Weinberg equilibrium stable: no mutation, no selection pressures, an isolated population, a large population, and random mating.

66. **Crossing over, which increases genetic diversity occurs during which stage(s)? (Competency 010)(Average)**

   A. telophase II in meiosis
   B. metaphase in mitosis
   C. interphase in both mitosis and meiosis
   D. prophase I in meiosis

Answer: D. prophase I in meiosis
During prophase I of meiosis, the replicated chromosomes condense and pair with their homologues in a process called synapsis. Crossing over, the exchange of genetic material between homologues to further increase diversity, occurs during prophase I.

67. **The biological species concept applies to …**
    (Competency 010)(Rigorous)

    A. asexual organisms.
    B. extinct organisms.
    C. sexual organisms.
    D. fossil organisms.

Answer: C. sexual organisms
The biological species concept states that a species is a reproductive community of populations that occupy a specific niche in nature. It focuses on reproductive isolation of populations as the primary criterion for recognition of species status. The biological species concept does not apply to organisms that are completely asexual in their reproduction, fossil organisms, or distinctive populations that hybridize.

68. **Reproductive isolation results in … (Competency 010)(Average)**

    A. extinction.
    B. migration.
    C. follilization.
    D. speciation.

Answer: D. speciation
Reproductive isolation is caused by any factor that impedes two species from producing viable, fertile hybrids. Reproductive isolation of populations is the primary criterion for recognition of species status.

69. **The Endosymbiotic theory states that … (Competency 011)(Rigorous)**

    A. eukaryotes arose from prokaryotes.
    B. animals evolved in close relationships with one another.
    C. prokaryotes arose from eukaryotes.
    D. life arose from inorganic compounds.

Answer: A. eukaryotes arose from prokaryotes
The Endosymbiotic theory of the origin of eukaryotes states that eukaryotes arose from symbiotic groups of prokaryotic cells. According to this theory, smaller prokaryotes lived within larger prokaryotic cells, eventually evolving into chloroplasts and mitochondria.

70. **Evolution occurs in ... (Competency 011)(Average)**

    A. individuals.
    B. populations.
    C. organ systems.
    D. cells.

Answer: B. populations
Evolution is a change in genotype over time. Gene frequencies shift and change from generation to generation. Populations evolve, individuals do not (and cannot) evolve.

71. **The wing of a bird, human arm, and whale flipper have the same bone structure. These are called ... Competency 012)(Average)**

    A. polymorphic structures.
    B. homologous structures.
    C. vestigial structures.
    D. analogous structures.

Answer: B. homologous structures
Homologous structures have the same genetic basis (leading to similar appearances), but are used for different functions.

72. **Which biome is the most prevalent on Earth? (Competency 012)(Easy)**

    A. marine
    B. desert
    C. savanna
    D. tundra

Answer: A. marine
The marine biome covers 75% of the Earth. This biome is further organized by the depth of water.

73. **The two major ways to determine taxonomic classification are (Competency 012)(Rigorous)**

    A. evolution and phylogeny.
    B. reproductive success and evolution.
    C. phylogeny and morphology.
    D. size and color.

Answer: C. phylogeny and morphology
Taxonomy is based on structure (morphology) and evolutionary relationships (phylogeny).

74. **Man's scientific name is *Homo sapiens*. Choose the proper classification beginning with kingdom and ending with order. (Competency 012)(Rigorous)**

    A. Animalia, Vertebrata, Mammalia, Primate, Hominidae
    B. Animalia, Vertebrata, Chordata, Mammalia, Primate
    C. Animalia, Chordata, Vertebrata, Mammalia, Primate
    D. Chordata, Vertebrata, Primate, Homo, sapiens

Answer: C. Animalia, Chordata, Vertebrata, Mammalia, Primate
The order of classification for humans is as follows: Kingdom, Animalia; Phylum, Chordata; Subphylum, Vertebrata; Class, Mammalia; Order, Primate; Family, Hominadae; Genus, Homo; Species, sapiens.

75. **Members of the same species (Competency 012)(Easy)**

    A. look identical.
    B. never change.
    C. reproduce successfully within their group.
    D. live in the same geographic location.

Answer: C. reproduce successfully within their group
Species are defined by the ability to successfully reproduce with members of their own kind.

76. **Water movement to the top of a twenty foot tree is most likely due to which principle? (Competency 013)(Average)**

    A. osmostic pressure
    B. xylem pressure
    C. capillarity
    D. transpiration

Answer: D. transpiration
Xylem is the tissue that transports water upward. Transpiration is the force that pulls the water upwards. Transpiration is the evaporation of water from leaves.

77. **What is not true of enzymes? (Competency 013)(Rigorous)**

    A. They are the most diverse of all proteins.
    B. They act on a substrate.
    C. They work over a wide pH range.
    D. They are temperature-dependent.

Answer: C. they work over a wide pH range
Enzymes generally work best within a very narrow pH range.

78. **What controls gas exchange on the bottom of a plant leaf? (Competency 013)(Average)**

    A. stomata
    B. epidermis
    C. collenchyma and schlerenchyma
    D. palisade mesophyll

Answer: A. stomata
Stomata provide openings on the underside of leaves for oxygen to move in or out of the plant and for carbon dioxide to move in.

79. **The function of the cardiovascular system is to ...**
(Competency 013)(Average)

   A. Move oxygenated blood around the body via a pump and tubes
   B. To oxygenate the blood through gas exchange.
   C. To act as an exocrine system
   D. To flush toxins out of the body

Answer: A. move oxygenated blood around the body via a pump and tubes
The cardiovascular system moves oxygenated blood around the body via the heart (a pump) and tubes (arteries and veins)

80. **Parts of the nervous system include all but the following ...**
(Competency 013)(Easy)

   A. brain
   B. spinal cord
   C. axons
   D. venules

Answer: D. venules
Venules are part of the circulatory system. The others are part of the nervous system.

81. **Which phylum accounts for 85% of all animal species?**
(Competency 013)(Average)

   A. Nematoda
   B. Chordata
   C. Arthropoda
   D. Cnidaria

Answer: C. Arthropoda
The arthropoda phylum consists of insects, crustaceans, and spiders. They are the largest group in the animal kingdom.

82. **Which is the correct statement regarding the human nervous system and the human endocrine system? (Competency 013)(Rigorous)**

    A. the nervous system maintains homeostasis whereas the endocrine system does not
    B. endocrine glands produce neurotransmitters whereas nerves produce hormones
    C. nerve signals travel on neurons whereas hormones travel through the blood
    D. the nervous system involves chemical transmission whereas the endocrine system does not

Answer: C. nerve signals travel on neurons whereas hormones travel through the blood
In the human nervous system, neurons carry nerve signals to and from the cell body. Endocrine glands produce hormones that are carried through the body in the bloodstream.

83. **A muscular adaptation to move food through the digestive system is Called ... (Competency 013)(Easy)**

    A. peristalsis.
    B. passive transport.
    C. voluntary action.
    D. bulk transport.

Answer: A. peristalsis
Peristalsis is a process of wave-like contractions. This process allows food to be carried down the pharynx and though the digestive tract.

84. **The role of neurotransmitters in nerve action is ... (Competency 013)(Rigorous)**

    A. to turn off the sodium pump.
    B. to turn off the calcium pump.
    C. to send impulses to neurons.
    D. to send impulses to the body.

Answer: A. to turn off the sodium pump
The neurotransmitters turn off the sodium pump, which results in depolarization of the membrane.

85. **Fertilization in humans usually occurs in the ...**
    (Competency 013)(Average)

    A. uterus.
    B. ovary.
    C. fallopian tubes.
    D. vagina.

Answer: C. fallopian tubes
Fertilization of the egg by the sperm normally occurs in the fallopian tube. The fertilized egg is then implanted on the uterine lining for development.

86. **All of the following are found in the dermis layer of skin except ...**
    (Competency 013)(Average)

    A. sweat glands.
    B. keratin.
    C. hair follicles.
    D. blood vessels.

Answer: B. keratin
Keratin is a water proofing protein found in the epidermis.

87. **Movement is possible by the action of muscles pulling on ...**
    (Competency 013)(Easy)

    A. skin.
    B. bones.
    C. joints.
    D. ligaments.

Answer: B. bones
The muscular system's function is for movement. Skeletal muscles are attached to bones by tendons and are responsible for their movement.

88. **All of the following are functions of the skin except ...**
   (Competency 013)(Average)

   A. storage.
   B. protection.
   C. sensation.
   D. regulation of temperature.

Answer: A. storage
Skin is a protective barrier against infection. It contains hair follicles that respond to sensation and it plays a role in thermoregulation.

89. **Hormones are essential to the regulation of reproduction. What organ is responsible for the release of hormones for sexual maturity? (Competency 013)(Average)**

   A. pituitary gland
   B. hypothalamus
   C. pancreas
   D. thyroid gland

Answer: B. hypothalamus
The hypothalamus begins secreting hormones that help mature the reproductive system and stimulate development of the secondary sex characteristics.

90. **A school age boy had the chicken pox as a baby. He will most likely not get this disease again because of ... (Competency 013)(Average)**

   A. passive immunity.
   B. vaccination.
   C. antibiotics.
   D. active immunity.

Answer: D. active immunity
Active immunity develops after recovery from an infectious disease, such as the chicken pox, or after vaccination. Passive immunity may be passed from one individual to another (from mother to nursing child).

91. The body's endocrine mechanisms are controlled by ...
   (Competency 013) (Average)

   A. feedback loops
   B. control molecules
   C. neurochemicals
   D. neurotransmitters

Answer: A. feedback loops
The body's mechanisms are controlled by feedback loops.

92. The most common neurotransmitter is ... (Competency 013)(Average)

   A. epinephrine
   B. serotonin
   C. acetylcholine
   D. norepinephrine

Answer: C. acetylcholine
The most common neurotransmitter is acetylcholine.

93. Homeostatic mechanisms in the body include all but the following ...
   (Competency 014)(Rigorous)

   A. Thermoregulation
   B. Excretion
   C. Respiration
   D. Osmoregulation

Answer: C. respiration
All but respiration are homeostatic mechanisms used by the body to achieve homeostasis.

94. **After sea turtles are hatched on the beach, they start the journey to the ocean. This is due to... (Competency 015)(Average)**

    A. innate behavior.
    B. territoriality.
    C. the tide.
    D. learned behavior.

Answer: A. innate behavior
Innate behavior is inborn or instinctual. The baby sea turtles did not learn from their mother. They immediately knew to head towards the shore once they hatched.

95. **Which term is not associated with the water cycle? (Competency 016)(Average)**

    A. precipitation
    B. transpiration
    C. fixation
    D. evaporation

Answer: C. fixation
Water is recycled through the processes of evaporation and precipitation. Transpiration is the evaporation of water from leaves. Fixation is not associated with the water cycle.

96. **All of the following are density independent factors that affect a population except ... (Competency 017)(Average)**

    A. temperature.
    B. rainfall.
    C. predation.
    D. soil nutrients.

Answer: C. predation
As a population increases, the competition for resources is intense and the growth rate declines. This is a density-dependent factor. An example of this would be predation. Density-independent factors affect the population regardless of its size. Examples of density-independent factors are rainfall, temperature, and soil nutrients.

97. **Which trophic level has the highest ecological efficiency? (Competency 017)(Average)**

   A. decomposers
   B. producers
   C. tertiary consumers
   D. secondary consumers

Answer: B. producers
The amount of energy that is transferred between trophic levels is called the ecological efficiency. The visual of this is represented in a pyramid of productivity. The producers have the greatest amount of energy and are at the bottom of this pyramid.

98. **In the growth of a population, the increase is exponential until carrying capacity is reached. This is represented by a(n) ... (Competency 018)(Rigorous)**

   A. S curve.
   B. J curve.
   C. M curve.
   D. L curve.

Answer: A. S curve
An exponentially growing population starts off with little change and then rapidly increases. The graphic representation of this growth curve has the appearance of a "J". However, as the carrying capacity of the exponentially growing population is reached, the growth rate begins to slow down and level off. The graphic representation of this growth curve has the appearance of an "S".

99. **Primary succession occurs after ... (Competency 018)(Rigorous)**

   A. nutrient enrichment.
   B. a forest fire.
   C. bare rock is exposed after a water table recedes.
   D. a housing development is built.

Answer: C. bare rock is exposed after a water table recedes
Primary succession occurs where life never existed before, such as flooded areas or a new volcanic island. It is only after the water recedes that the rock is able to support new life.

100. A clownfish is protected by the sea anemone's tentacles. In turn, the anemone receives uneaten food from the clownfish. This is an example of … (Competency 018)(Rigorous)

    A. mutualism.
    B. parasitism.
    C. commensalisms.
    D. competition.

Answer: A. mutualism
Neither the clownfish nor the anemone cause harmful effects towards one another and they both benefit from their relationship. Mutualism is when two species that occupy a similar space benefit from their relationship.

CPSIA information can be obtained
at www.ICGtesting.com
Printed in the USA
BVOW07s1356301216

472117BV00010B/21/P